If I'm So Smart,

Why Can't I Get Rid of This Clutter?

ALSO BY THE AUTHOR

"Stepping Stones for Success, Experts Share Strategies for Mastering Business, Life & Relationships"

"Clutter Free and Clear: Take Charge of Your Time and Space, A How-to-Book to Simplify Your Life"

"GPS (Goals & Proven Strategies) for Success... From the Industry's Leading Experts" (Spring 2011)

"Start Where You Stand, Finding Your True Worth in the Life/Work Balance" (Spring 2011) A companion guide/workbook to GPS.

If I'm So Smart,

Why Can't I Get Rid of This Clutter?

Tools To Get It Done!

Sallie Felton

Journey Grrrl

PUBLISHING

Published by Journey Grrrl Publishing, Washington DC an imprint of Becoming Journey, LLC

If I'm So Smart, Journey Grrrl Publishing, and the road meets the horizon design are registered trademarks of Becoming Journey, LLC.

ISBN-13: 978-1-9369-8400-8

Library of Congress Number: 2011931368

Design by Ann Alger

Desktop Publishing by Poodles Doodles

How to get your Free Gifts!

As a way of saying thanks for buying *If I'm So Smart, Why Can't I Get Rid of This Clutter?,* we are pleased to offer you some **FREE Gifts** to accompany the book.

Visit www.SoSmartOnline.com/Clutter to claim your free gifts today.

Throughout the book, author Sallie Felton offers practical tools for incorporating her approach into your life. We've selected a few of our favorites and made them available for you to download, print and try out. When you register, you'll receive all the documents in a single bundle.

Whether you have read *If I'm So Smart, Why Can't I Get Rid of This Clutter?* or not, these resources are free gifts from the author to you.

Here are some highlights of what you'll get:

- Practical Go-To Storage Solutions: a list of Sallie's favorite stores and resources for products to help you get organized
- "Honey-We-Do" List Template: Print out your own template and make progress on your own to-do list
- Holiday Gift List Template: Print out your own and get organized around gift-giving
- Holiday Grocery List: A complete shopping list for your big holiday event
- Sallie's List of Clutter Tips: A compiled list of Sallie's most popular Clutter tips
- Interview with Author and Clutter Expert Sallie Felton: Hear what Sallie has to say about her book

Go to www.SoSmartOnline.com/Clutter to download your free gifts today!

Journey Grrrl
PUBLISHING

I dedicate this book to all of my past, present and future clients who have challenged me to think outside of all those boxes in the attic in order to find new ways to de-clutter. Each of you has brought to me the vision of a more peaceful, stress-free and organized life. It is because of you, that this book has been written. Your humor and your frustrations, but most of all

your unique ways of looking at the world
are
the gifts I take from you.

YOU HAVE PROVEN THAT WE CAN ALL CONQUER CLUTTER!

ACKNOWLEDGEMENTS

Although writing is, by and large, a solitary pursuit, I had the great fortune while working on this project to receive inspiration, insight and support from several individuals without whom this book would have never come to light.

To my publisher, Angela Lauria - who called me out of the blue with the idea for this book—you piqued my interest with this project, convinced me I could get this book written in a mere three months and were there to support me 24/7 throughout this journey. We got it done!

To Penny Reynolds, my virtual assistant, you helped me stay on top of things, brought your keen eye to what needed correcting and kept me on track, no matter how crazy things got at times. You have no idea how grateful I am for your skills as well as your friendship.

To Maureen Cidzik, your ability to revise and rewrite is a talent I so much admire and envy. Your sense of organization and systematic approach to getting things done is remarkable. Your readiness and willingness to be an early reader of this book and take on the project is very much appreciated. Without you I would still have my fingers on the keyboard, thank you dear friend.

I would not be who I am today—neither would this book have been written—without my "emotional" mother, Hazel Young. She nurtured me and my sisters throughout our childhoods and, with her smile, gentle nature and kindness, radiated that warmth to everyone who was ever in her presence. When I hear the phrases "kindness begets kindness" and "start where you stand," it's her voice who speaks those words. They have become the foundation of my life and my work.

To my sisters Nina, Taffy, Gretchen and Dana who shower me with kindness, unconditional love and laughter; you four are my best friends! I love you each dearly.

To my husband, Conway, who has been my best friend, soul mate and companion for more than 36 years: You have wrapped me with constant love, support and encouragement. Your love and stability have brought me to where I am now. I thank you for believing in my dreams and in me.

Last, but not least, I want to thank my children: Corey, Sarah, and Taylor—for your adventurous natures, wit, sparkle, support and love for one another. You are each so dear to my heart. May you always follow your passions and your wings be forever strong. Thank you for encouraging me to continue with this book (and de-cluttering your rooms).

If I'm So Smart,
Why Can't I Get Rid of This Clutter?

Contents

INTRODUCTION

*"You can be, have, or achieve anything you desire
as soon as you decide to be, have, or achieve it. It's your choice."*

Alan Underkofler

Let's face it; everyone has clutter to some degree or another! It's <u>how</u> you deal with the clutter that makes the difference between conquering your clutter and allowing your clutter to conquer you.

If you have picked up this book, it must have spoken to you in some way. Maybe the word CLUTTER caught your eye or prompted your inner voice to tell you to take a closer look. Maybe you've discovered that your clutter—all that "stuff" that surrounds you—is sapping your strength, perhaps even to the point where it's taken over nearly every aspect of your life.

If any of this sounds familiar, let me ask you a few thought-provoking questions designed to evoke your self-awareness:

- If you close your eyes and wave a magic wand, how would you **envision** your life to be without clutter?
- What would it **FEEL** like to remove some or all of that clutter from your life?
- What would letting go of this "stuff" **give** you?
- How would your **life** be different without clutter?
- If you knew you could **not fail** with your de-cluttering, how would you go about it?

Answering these questions is your very first step toward conquering clutter. Before you read the following chapters, take out your journal and write down how you would answer these questions, as candidly and poignantly as you can. No one is looking over your shoulder; you won't be graded or judged on what you write. However, by being as honest as you can be, you'll set the stage for this process of de-cluttering to be more empowering than you ever dreamed.

Clutter shows up in our lives in a variety of ways and, contrary to what you might believe, it's made up of more than the mess in the places we live—clutter also shows up in our inner homes inside our minds and our hearts.

In the first part of this book, we're going to take a close look at the three forms of clutter we all deal with—mental, physical and emotional—and how they each affect us all.

For example, does the chatter in your head never slow down? Does your mind never grow still? Are you constantly going over your to-do list in your head to the point that even when your body is exhausted, your brain just keeps going and you never feel rested or focused? That's mental clutter screaming at you, loud and clear.

What about your physical space? Is the clutter threatening to suck you in? Can you find things when you need them? Are you able to move freely about each room or are you knee-deep in "stuff" everywhere you turn? When our living space, which should provide shelter, nurture us and provide refuge, is cluttered, it can lead to feelings of frustration, irritation, overwhelming unrest and shame.

Emotional clutter is the feelings, issues and fears we haven't processed or released. It can be as simple as feeling you have no time for yourself, an unresolved conflict that needs attention or a deeper fear of change. Whatever we're holding onto in our hearts, drains our energy and unconsciously drives our behaviors. Residing deep within our hearts, emotional clutter plays a powerful role in our health and well-being.

In the pages that follow, I'll cover tried-and-true methods that will teach you how to clear all three forms of clutter and provide you with simple and practical tools and tips to guide you through the de-cluttering process. Drawing from my own experiences and those of my clients (past and present), you'll learn that you're not alone with your clutter issues and that you have absolutely nothing to be ashamed about.

Even if you have great difficulty letting go, I'll show you, step by step, how you can learn to take control of your clutter and work through the emotional ties by which you're bound to "stuff." Together, we'll loosen the hold your clutter has on you and through it all, I'll be cheering you on, helping you to stay motivated and celebrate each and every one of your successes along the way.

In Chapter One, I'll introduce you further to the three forms of clutter and how they affect us all and share a personal story of how, in 2008, I made a public declaration on my blog to de-clutter my entire house, top to bottom and inside and out. In these blog excerpts you'll gain a sense of why it's important to have a vision or intention behind de-cluttering and see how I approached this massive goal, which was so daunting at times, it felt as though I were climbing Mt. Everest wearing flip-flops with an empty pack and no gear. You'll also see how effective being accountable to my blog readers kept me on track, even at my lowest points.

In Chapter Two, we're going to take a closer look at mental clutter and see what my de-cluttering workshop participants have had to say about theirs over the years. Clutter often begins from the inside, working its way out, but that's not always the case. The exercises in this chapter are designed to help you identify your own brand of mental clutter and put a plan in place to reduce your mental load, improve your focus and increase your productivity.

We'll tackle physical clutter in Chapter Three—the most common form of clutter—and discuss at length the power it has to take over our lives and negatively impact our health and overall well-being. Whether you're dealing with a single overcrowded guest room or a whole house full of clutter, I'll show you, room by room, how you can begin to take your power back and return to owning your things rather than having them own you.

I'll speak directly from the heart in Chapter Four and share my personal stories of how I worked through the process of clearing some specific emotional clutter out of my life (Hint: The magic lies in learning to let go.) Emotional clutter is perhaps the most difficult to clear, but if we move slowly and treat ourselves tenderly and with love, it can be done one heartbeat at a time.

In Chapter Five, we're going to put a value on your clutter—a LIFE value. Whether you're holding onto mental, physical or emotional clutter (and most of us hold onto all three kinds), you pay a price. The exercises in this chapter will show you exactly what your clutter is costing you. You'll find tools to help you recognize what you're feeling, connect you to each of these feelings, respect them and take appropriate action to transform them.

You've probably heard before that we create our lives based on the thoughts we think. In other words, we are what we believe (positive or negative). Chapter Six will help you unearth the beliefs you have about yourself and teach you how to turn the negative, self-defeating ones into empowering affirmations. If you're stuck in a rut, believe you can't change, feel alone or that you're "less than" anything, you'll want to pay particular attention to this chapter—it's a life changer. The more self-aware you become, the more easily you can change your attitude and your belief system. After all, you are the pilot of your plane and only you can change your course. **You DO have choices!**

It's my belief that self care and nurturing are among the most important and life-affirming gifts we can give to ourselves. Too often we push ourselves, day in and day out, to do more, give more and achieve more. To what end? If we don't make time to take care of ourselves - to re-energize and re-vitalize ourselves - we make it impossible to do, give or achieve our best. So what will it take to make yourself a priority and how do you begin to do that? We'll cover this and more in Chapter Seven.

Then, get ready to TAKE ACTION. Chapter Eight is where you're going to learn how to put a plan in place and be accountable for bringing life to your vision and creating the future you want. Here's where we put all of the pieces in this book together and see what happens when we commit to being responsible for ourselves and our choices, staying focused on our goals and keeping our ultimate vision in clear view. We'll do this in a way that builds confidence, makes room for life's unpredictable ways and sets you up for nothing less than success.

Finally, in Chapter Nine, we're going to spend some time looking at how we can maintain our vision and goals during that most stressful time of year—the holiday season. I wasn't sure at first, that I would include this chapter in the book, but the more I thought about it, the more I realized this time of year is ripe for all forms of clutter to take a stronger hold. Not only will the tools in this chapter help you navigate the holidays with more ease and less stress, they'll help set the stage for a de-cluttered entry into the new year that follows.

Lastly, at the back of the book you'll find lists of recommended reading, resources and websites to consult throughout your journey.

So now, find a quiet place, treat yourself to your favorite beverage and let's get started. There is never a better time than the present.

> *"Life can be found only in the present moment. The past is gone, the future is not yet here, and if we do not go back to ourselves in the present moment, we cannot be in touch with life."*

Thich Nhat Hanh

If I'm So Smart,

Why Can't I Get Rid of This Clutter?

CHAPTER ONE
"Are You Kidding, There are Three?"

"When considering change, remember — there is an emotional connection necessary for people to commit to new ways."

Stacy Aaron

WHAT IS CLUTTER?

When you think about clutter, what comes to mind? You might think it's just the physical stuff—on your dining-room table, stored out of sight in your attic or taking over your car. Or maybe you think about the paperwork piling up on your desk that needs to be filed, how you can't ever seem to find what you're looking for or how you haven't seen the surface of your kitchen counters (aka, "magic magnets") in a while.

The truth is: Clutter shows up in our lives in three ways—mentally, physically and emotionally. Each area plays an important role in our well-being and none of them stands alone.

So if you are feeling disorganized and/or unproductive, which form of clutter do you start with first? Is it your emotional clutter that stops you from letting go of your physical clutter or is your physical clutter responsible for the mental clutter?

When I work with clients on clutter issues, these are the questions I ask them to help zero in on what kind of clutter we're dealing with:

- What is it like to get up in the morning and face your clutter?
- Where do you have clutter in your life?
- Where do you see your clutter?
- Where is it spinning in your head?
- Where do you feel your clutter?
- Where do you feel you are the most disorganized?
- We know clutter works from the inside out, how is it affecting you?

Finally, I'll ask them, "Which form of clutter is the most difficult for you to start clearing?" The response, nine times out of 10, is "all three." Now, we're getting somewhere and all we have to do is agree to begin. And now is the time to be kinder to yourself and to think more positively.

At the end of this chapter, I'll share with you my own personal story and how I used the same tools I'm giving you here to de-clutter my own house - literally and figuratively - over the course of a year.

"I believe if you stir up mindful clutter,
You will have a recipe for a potent stew.
By learning which herbs and spices to use,
You create a gourmet feast."

Sallie Felton

TOOL #1

RECOGNIZING MENTAL CLUTTER

When I ask audiences, "What's the one thing you'd like to have come into your life?" Their first answer is "More money." The second is "More balance in my life." "What kind of balance?" "More time for friends and family and less stress at work," they add. The third, almost without fail is, "Less clutter."

To find real balance, we have to look at all facets to our lives, including clutter and the various ways it shows up in our lives and our psyches.

It's no wonder—we live in an era that moves at warp speed. From drive-thru and pick-up windows to Skype and smartphones, we have an abundance of information at our fingertips, ready for consumption in seconds. So it's also assumed or implied that just because information comes in at the speed of the light, we'll respond to that information the same way—in seconds.

What do you think this does to your body, mind and spirit? It's a recipe for an over-stressed, over-scheduled, over-exhausted and over-stimulated self. Throw all of these requests, demands and obligations into the blender, puree at high speed and what's the result? Dis-ease. Mental, physical and emotional stresses have to go somewhere and if we don't find outlets for them, we'll direct them inward, unconsciously.

As amazing as it sounds, we actually do get to control what comes into and goes out of our lives. What a concept!

I believe mental clutter is the "what I didn't do," "what I need to do," and "what I should be doing," running on a nonstop loop in our heads.

Multi-taskers are skilled at clearing mental clutter. Surgeons in disguise, they thrive on deadlines, dissecting every task that needs to be done, checking each item twice before crossing it off their list. Their tools of choice are

Blackberries, calendars, day planners, notebooks, pencils and pens. The process they follow is backed by a strong sense of organization.

For the rest of us, it's more like we're waging battle against a never-ending flow of information streaming into our minds, where it gets stuck. If this sounds like you, take heart. Recognizing that you've got a problem with mental clutter is the first step in beginning to rid yourself of this excess baggage before it begins to seep into the rest of your life.

> *"I think we all have a little voice inside us that will guide us...*
> *If we shut out all the noise and clutter from our lives and listen to*
> *that voice, it will tell us the right thing to do."*
>
> **Christopher Reeve**

TOOL #2

RECOGNIZING PHYSICAL CLUTTER

The second form of clutter is the one we all think of when we hear the word. It's our physical clutter, all that extra and VISIBLE stuff that piles up around us and takes over our work and living environments.

It's easier to identify: newspapers, magazines, mail, catalogues, paperwork, piles of clothing, overflowing closets, shoes on the floor, tools laying this way and that, all over the basement or garage, mixed in with holiday decorations.

When you read that description of physical clutter, how does it make you feel? Anxious? Overwhelmed? Shameful? Have you ever stopped to think what the emotional price of having physical clutter costs you?

I know for me, if my office is not somewhat tidy, I feel fragmented and my productivity decreases; my thinking gets cloudy, I start to lag behind on my to-do list and I'm definitely not firing on all cylinders I need to be.

Physical clutter affects different people in different ways. Spend a few moments thinking about how you react to it. What happens when you take a good look at all that stuff? Do you feel a pit form in your stomach? Does it grate on your nerves? Maybe you just want to close the door and run. Out of sight, out of mind, right? Wrong. What takes up space in our physical environment naturally takes up space our in head (cleaning and organization need to get done) and in our hearts (negative self-talk).

"You will find it easier to do a single, small piece of a large project than to start on the whole job."

Brian Tracy

TOOL #3

RECOGNIZING EMOTIONAL CLUTTER

Emotional clutter comes straight from the heart. It includes the feelings surrounding past and present issues we haven't yet processed, worked through, nurtured or released. Emotional clutter is judgment (of self and others), expectation, unresolved conflicts (with self and others) and self-defeating behaviors, like perfectionism.

I believe emotional clutter lives in the very center of the heart, affecting our sense of self and our self-esteem. Symptoms of emotional clutter can range from feeling over-stressed and overburdened to simply feeling imbalanced. These symptoms manifest into conditions like low productivity, inefficiency and lack of effectiveness. They can also show up as fear, pain, sadness, frustration or anger.

When you're trying to determine if you're dealing with emotional clutter issues, ask yourself:

- Is there someone you feel needs forgiveness or you feel you can't forgive?
- Are you avoiding confrontation?
- Have you let a personal or professional issue go too long unaddressed?

When you know the answers, spend a few minutes thinking about how these situations affect you emotionally. How strong a grip do they have on you? What role do they play in keeping you from being at peace?

"Say no to anything that is not a high-value use of your time and your life."

Brian Tracy

TOOL #4

"COACHES HAVE CLUTTER TOO"

Many times over the years, I've been asked:

- How do you stay focused and maintain the momentum to complete a task or reach a goal?
- How do you not get distracted?
- How do you set yourself up for success vs. failure so you'll actually begin?

In 2008, I decided to turn my coaching skills on myself and make the experience public by writing about it on my blog. At that point, my children were grown and had fled the nest, leaving my husband and me with a large, empty house that needed to function differently now that it was just the two of us.

Following are excerpts from my blog that show you how I got started and continued to move forward, even when it proved challenging.

JANUARY 23, 2008

MY TURN

I am throwing the gauntlet down and making a pledge to myself. By January 28, I am going to post my New Year Resolutions for 2008 and everything I would like to complete by the end of the year....no matter how large or small.

I am going to write on this blog each day or week - should technology and the newness of this blog not fail me - all of my failures, disappointments, wins, successes and tips that I used to complete my goals. Accountability is key!

What better way to show others of you out there what can be accomplished by setting the example? Through thick or thin, one way or another my list will be ticked off line by line. So stay tuned...six days until I unveil my own goals...

...Yikes, what have I gotten myself into?!

JANUARY 23, 2008
BABY STEPS

Ok, now that the gauntlet is down and I'm going to reveal to the world what my New Year's goals/resolutions will be, let me say that in making this list, it will be long because I'm giving myself a year to complete it.

There will be more than 15 de-cluttering tasks, but less than 25, I hope. There will be some tasks that need more time allocated than others, however, everything will be listed.

Here is what I plan to do first:

* List will be created.

* Beside each task or job will be how much time I believe will be needed for me to complete it.

JANUARY 28, 2008
MY GOALS FOR DE-CLUTTERING

Today is January 28, the day I promised that I would give you my goals for the year 2008. But before I do that, I want to answer the question, "What is the most important aspect of making a goal?" And the answer is, "That you show up and be accountable for taking action, whether it is daily, weekly or monthly." So here I am, accountable to all of my readers and my radio listeners.

My goals for the year appear in random order for a reason—they're simply the result of brainstorming everything I would like to accomplish during this year. Some goals are loftier than others, but it does not matter. What matters is how they get done and what plan is in place to make them happen.

MY GOALS FOR 2008

1. Redo filing system for the business
2. Update personal files
3. Shred unnecessary health files...my kids', my parents', my husband's and mine
4. Make new website for ROCKING HORSE (my holiday items company)

5. Clean out every closet in the house: the kids', ours, laundry room, bathrooms, kitchen, workshop, living room, dining room, office, den, linen closet and the basement. (No, we don't have an attic—thank goodness!)

6. Organize all the photographs from the past 14 years and put them in: albums? On CDs? Or give to kids?

7. Recycle and donate to Salvation Army, veterans, consignment shops, etc.

8. Sell hot tub

9. Paint kitchen, den, back hall

10. Select, buy new couches for den

11. Choose fabric for club chairs and reupholster

12. Clean out above the garage

13. Clean out tool shed

14. Clean out loft above the back-hall

15. Replace screens in office

16. Cut back trees and bushes from storm damage

17. Simplify two perennial garden beds

18. Plant vegetable garden

19. Redo stone wall

20. Sort through EVERY drawer in the house, simplify

21. Shred outdated house files

22. Go through every file in all the file cabinets: shred, simplify, combine

23. Give away furniture that no longer suits our needs

24. Straighten out all items on the walls in the garage

25. Recycle; dispose of all unused paint environmentally

26. Clear, sort every shelf in the house

That does it for now. I'm sure I've forgotten some things, but can add on as time goes by.

Tomorrow I will show you how to breakdown and prioritize.

JANUARY 29, 2008
PERSONAL GOALS

OK, it was just before the stroke of midnight last night on January 28 when I realized that I didn't include my **personal goals for 2008**. Here goes:

1. Schedule and make time with old friends
2. Increase exercise routine...i.e. walk with the dog
3. Recreate good habits...take time to eat breakfast and not on the fly
4. Take a Yoga class
5. Re-design early morning routine...make habit-forming

JANUARY 30, 2008
PRIORITIZING

I awoke this morning with the thought that I needed to prioritize my list of goals for 2008. But before that one more thing needs to happen: We need to look at the list and be S.M.A.R.T.

S stands for Simple and Specific

M stands for Measureable

A stands for Attainable

R stands for Realistic

T stands for Time-oriented

Tomorrow I will show you how this works.

FEBRUARY 1, 2008
HOW TO BEGIN

Yesterday, I introduced you to the **S.M.A.R.T.** goals. Here is a review:

S stands for Simple and Specific. When you outline your goals, make sure they are simple and be specific about what you want to get done.

For instance, I want to do #2 of my list, update my personal files. What do I mean by that? Being specific, it means I want to:

- Discard all those papers that are not relevant anymore.

- Put those papers that I wish to keep in newer files, if applicable. For example: if I have old report cards that belong to my eldest son, who is now 27, I think it's time that he has his own specific box labeled with his name on it and the contents of that box listed. No need for me to hold onto those report cards.

When I go through his folder, I will sort out all the most important reports and comments from his teachers. I need not hold on to every homework assignment or note that came home. All of those unnecessary papers will be shredded. I have kept up with this task over the years, but sometimes it is best to do a complete review.

M stands for Measurable. Is this a task that can be measured? How long will it take me? How will I feel when this is completed? The answer is, "I'll feel great," because I am one-third of the way there going through my adult children's files. It is important to me to complete this goal because it cleans out the file drawer of unnecessary material and allows something else to come into my life. Possibly travel from discovering brochures I've saved of places we would like to visit!

A stands for Attainable. Can this be attained? YOU BET! How? I can easily bring the files into the family room and work on them while watching the nightly news. Becoming a multi-tasker is not all bad.

R stands for Realistic. Is it? ABSOLUTELY! This is something I could do each night until it is completed. Break it down, one file each night for 7 nights…that's 7 folders done.

T stands for Time-Oriented. The big question is always, "When are you going to do it?" Am I going to make excuses not to? What complaints about the task(s) will come to the surface? Whatever they are, they're not valid—just excuses.

I'm going to start tonight with Corey's school files. The news is on and I can get started right now. How can any goal be reached if I don't even begin?

So I have marked in my calendar from 6-7pm, "Go through Kids' personal files," I am showing up and being accountable.

How long do I think this will take me? Realistically? Two nights. One-hour each. Two hours of TV news listening and shredding at the same time. I will let you know the results of one night tomorrow.

FEBRUARY 4, 2008
FURIOUSLY FILING

And you thought that I was not doing anything!!! Why, because I have not written for a while? Never, not me. I want to tell you that the other night I collected all the personal files for two of our three adult children containing elementary school, high school and college stuff. When I lifted the boxes, my first thought was, "Oh my gosh, this box is so heavy—there is going to be so much to do."

Here is what happened: With a cup of coffee, a fire in the fireplace, and the news at hand, I was able to get through that box.

What am I learning from this?

I was very aware of how heavy the box of files felt as I carried it. Metaphorically speaking, it weighed on my shoulders as well. It was exciting to see the pile of discarded papers piling up...higher and higher! There was a real jolt of accomplishment and something that I had wanted to finish for such a long time. When all was completed, the remaining folders were lighter...readily returned to the file cabinet for my adult children to inherit. Yeah me!

FEBRUARY 7, 2008
PRIORITIZING AND COMBINING GOALS

Last night before I taught my "Conquer Clutter" class, I sat in the den with my husband watching the news. Knowing that I needed to keep whittling away at the warranty, appliances and vacation files, I found the time sitting by the fire to be a masterful way of multi-tasking.

Job done. Length of time? One hour. Files back into the file drawer, each appropriately labeled on the outside with either: "Household, Pets, Kids, Travel, Airlines, Important Documents, Computer."

What am I learning from this?

When trying to accomplish a task that I don't particularly like to do, especially the warranty and appliance folders (can't get more boring than those), I felt more energized to be in the company of someone else. My husband and dog were there, which made the chore less of a drudgery.

How to Prioritize/Combine Goals:

Here's the thinking process I applied to prioritizing and combining my own goals for the year:

- What season are you in...What can be done now?

- What can you do inside of your house that you can't do outside?

- Make a notation by your goals of the month this will be done.

- If there is a repair, for which season do you need it for?
  For example: screens needing repair? Fix in the winter, ready for the summer. Bet your repair bill will be even cheaper!!!

- Paint rooms, do in the winter: less expensive and painters are looking for inside jobs.

- Think of spring cleaning: fresh...renewed...go through closets and drawers.

- Outside work waits until the late spring, like me if you live in the Northeast.

I review my list and make a notation of what needs to be finished by a certain SEASON. For example, item #15, screens in my office. What a perfect time now to call and have them fixed, as I don't open up the windows up here in the Northeast during the winter. Therefore, I make a notation of the Month that these will be repaired; March. They will all set and ready to go in the Spring.

Notice that some of the items can be done in the summer. #12, **garage** is not going to be cleaned or sorted through in -2 degree winter weather; I am hearty, but it is NOT my priority to freeze out there. Therefore, I make a notation next to garage, do in the early summer months: May, June or early July. #24 and #25 will be completed with the garage at the same-time. #13, tool shed to be cleaned out, same method applies, early summer. Again it can be done even in the rain. These two jobs can be done one after the other.

NOW I AM CELEBRATING MY ACCOMPLISHMENTS AND WINS!

And I'm taking the weekend off.

What's Next:

1. #29 is scheduled

2. Making time for old friend

3. #30 redesign early morning routine...make habit-forming

FEBRUARY 7, 2008
FURIOUSLY FINISHING, PART II

ONE GROUP DOWN!!! As of last night, I finished our youngest child's personal folder/files. It felt great to be able to have completed this task. I lightened the load; and the file cabinet actually breathes!

What am I learning from this?

When first opening the file drawer and seeing all the files that deal with our three kids, immediately I instinctively wanted to shut it. There was **so much** and **I waited** and **procrastinated** for this long, what difference would another couple of years make?

Does that sound familiar? Whose voice is that?

My inner critic—the inner critic we all have. So what do we do? Let the inner critic know this is something you have wanted to tackle and accomplish for a long time. Look to the vision...the end result; Visualize what this file drawer will look like and how it is going to make you feel. Now with piles of paper gone, my kids will appreciate it when I give them their own THINNER files back someday....very soon!

FEBRUARY 26, 2008
VACATION OVER, BACK TO WORK

You must think that I have been slacking off for the past two weeks. Well, to tell you the truth, the first week I was on vacation with my adult sons and daughter...the second week, I'm getting back on schedule.

While I was away from the blog, I made a list of what habits that I want to change.

The first was to re-design my morning routine and make myself commit to this, even when I'm distracted by other things I'd like to do.

Job Done. First thing was simply to make sure that our bed was made in the morning. Simple, yes, but not when I have a husband who likes to plop back on top of the bed to read his book before he heads out to work. That can be challenging.

What am I learning from this?

I timed myself; it would take me exactly 3 minutes to make the bed. Why were these three minutes so hard to come by? There are so many other things I'd rather do. But I noticed, when the bed wasn't made, I never quite felt put together. You know what I mean, when something's just not right.

I have made it a point now for the past week to get up and not leave our room until the bed is made. I have to confess that it does make a difference in my attitude for the day. Knowing that I accomplished something that has been so hard for me to recommit to, I'll keep working on it and it will become a habit.

What's Next:

Tomorrow, another look at the goals...and habits, working at whittling away the files.

MARCH 3, 2008
STRUGGLING

This has been a long and sad week for me. A very dear friend and my old tennis coach died of cancer this past week. To say that I have felt down is an understatement. I apologize for the delay in logging and posting my accomplishments.

As I write this I'm having an "AH-HA" moment. While visiting Rick in his Hospice room, I was struck that there he was surrounded by friends and family, a plethora of get-well cards, drawings from his grandchildren and pictures of his loved ones—did he need anything more?

Did he *need* his old tennis racket? Did he *need* all the extra socks, shoes, towels and did he *need* all those trophies to remind himself or others of his accomplishments? No! He *needed* what was most precious…family and friends.

I was reminded again when we leave this world we take with us three of the greatest gifts: our memories, our wisdom and our experience. And if we are truly wealthy…the gift of love.

What am I learning from this?

Sometimes when we make a promise to others and want to be accountable for completing that task, life gets in the way.
Case in point, the death of my dear friend. How has it affected me and my goals…I have felt tired, withdrawn and not my usual upbeat self. This past Sunday, I participated in a wonderful conference celebrating women and their empowerment. The gathering was fruitful, amazing to watch, but I was not at my very best. My mind kept jumping back to Rick, knowing there was a celebration of his life taking place that day and I was not able to be there. However, I am attending his funeral later today.

I share this with you because it goes to show that things do get in our way of progress and taking action. Situations happen that we have no control over, however, they're not a reason to jump ship and give up on a goal. Yes, my week was full of lows, but it did not deter me from continuing on, little by little, to regain the steam of the earlier weeks. Remember, one step at a time…be kind to yourself.

What got done:

#15, Replace Screens is done! We are all ready for the Spring.

#30, Changing Bad Habits…yes, I continue to jump out of bed, make it and begin my day as if the bow on the present was beautifully tied. It feels more complete to me…and it is becoming a better habit.

#7, Took items to the Consignment shop last couple of weeks…and I received a check in the mail. SWEET! Time to celebrate.

#2, 21, 22, Files: discarded to the recycling pile all unneeded paint charts from my "Paint" file; kept any important info from "My Computer" file; only one more file left to go in the two long file drawer cabinet… "House" files…here we go!

What's Next:

#5, Think I will begin to go through each of the closets one by one... Spring is coming and it will feel good to recycle, remove and regain space.
It is nice to be able to vary the goals from week to week. I can still continue to work on the paper filing again during the evening hours while watching the news. That has worked well for me and it has not become troublesome.

#9, Calling painters to get estimates to paint the kitchen, den and back hall. Better to do it now when the painters are not able to head outside for summer jobs.

MARCH 19, 2008
ONE STEP AT A TIME

Can't believe that my last entry was almost two weeks ago, but then again, yes, I can.

Life can play funny tricks on us. I never thought I would feel so drained by the death of my former coach and friend Rick.

So here I am now, pulling up the boot straps and putting one foot in front of the other. ONE STEP AT A TIME. I am being kind to myself and doing what it is that I can with the energy that I have left at the end of the day.

How?

I Start Where I Stand. Even if it is an inch...I just do a little bit. Better to do something than nothing at all. That just breeds frustration, guilt and stirs up the inner critic.

What got done:

#21, Shred unwanted house files..........DONE, DONE, DONE! Realistically, it took me two weeks to get through this group of files. I found estimates from work to be done on the house going back to 1977.

#1, Redo filing system for the business... half way done...Great to sit by the fire and wade through these files that have not been tended to since 2004. Reorganized, consolidated, recycled and reused back sides of paper.

#7, Took unneeded items to an auction house and will receive a check this week...SWEET!

What's Next:

I am going to finish #1 goal tonight..."YIPEEEEEEEEEEEEEEE," another one down! Start on #5...cleaning out every closet in the house.

MARCH 29, 2008
FEELING LIGHTER!

GOALS COMPLETED TO DATE:

#s 1, 2, 3, 7 (ongoing), 15, 21, 22, 26, 30

What am I learning from this?

I am amazed that nine of my goals for 2008 have already been completed. That is nine out of 30!! Not bad and it's only March. The momentum continues and as I gather the next group of goals, I find myself like a steam engine...this can be contagious.

What got done:

#1, Re-doing my entire filing system for my business is now COMPLETED! Recycled eight paper bags of paper!

#7, Taking those unneeded items to be donated or list on www.freecycle.org are constantly being tended too. Posted items on freecycle and they were gone in 24 hours...

What's Next:

Have begun to tackle one shelf at a time in my office. By tonight, I should be finished.

Living room, downstairs bathroom, dining room will be next...one shelf, one draw, one closet at a time.

APRIL 1, 2008
I'M ON A ROLL!

In the past week I have:

Collated, hole-punched all articles and photos of our son's last five years on the professional freeskiing circuit. This has been something that I have wanted to complete for so long, but kept putting it off because it looked so daunting. And now here it is, labeled with tabs, so any other information can be easily entered. What a great feeling!!!

All business files are completely done and each night before I leave the office the paper is filed. This is creating a good habit and *I thought I couldn't do it!!!*

All books in my office have been organized by author's name and categorized by topics, which means my office is completed.

Tackled one of the cabinets in the living room. I stored financial papers, which are no longer necessary to keep. Shredded them all. One cabinet down...three more to go.

Put four items on the freecycle list in the morning. By the afternoon, they were all gone.

What am I learning from this?

One Step At A Time...I know I keep saying that, but it is true. A little bit...just being able to reorganize all the books in my office was a huge undertaking. But I did one shelf at a time; less daunting to me than to take all the books out and see them in a huge pile. Visually that may have done me in. So figure out what works best for YOU.

What's Next:

Today is a warmer day, so I am going out into the Tool Shed, Goal #13, and working at freecycling all those extra garden tools and supplies I do not need. If you don't want to freecycle use Craigslist.org. But know there are people out there who could use what you no longer need. How many of the SAME shovels do you really need!

Will tackle another cabinet in the living room.

APRIL 11, 2008

SPRING FEVER FRENZY

LISTS OF GOALS COMPLETED TO DATE:

#s 1, 2, 3, 7, 15, 21, 22, 26, 30

In the past week I have:

1. Kept my desk free and clear of "breeding" piles of papers.
2. No clutter is left on the kitchen or dining room tables, NOTHING!
3. Freecycled all the old record albums that I have not listened to in 30 years. So, why did I save them? Memories!
4. Dug out the potting shed and the tool shed.
5. Raked out all the gardens and simplified.

What am I learning from this?

When it came to my record albums, I kept them because they reminded me of my youth... great days and freedom of responsibility. However, I still can hear many of those songs on the radio today. Being a creature who does like change, having them sprinkled amongst today's "listening pleasures" are OK with me. I still have all the memories and no one can ever take those away!

What's Next:

1. Finish up on the potting shed.
2. Do one more cabinet in the living room...three to go.
3. UGH...better do the loft above the mudroom before the painters get here. That will be an undertaking unto itself.

APRIL 23, 2008

DO THE RIGHT TASKS AT THE RIGHT TIME

LISTS OF GOALS COMPLETED TO DATE:

#s 1, 2, 3, 7, 8, 9, 13, 15, 16, 17, 21, 22, 26, 30

What got done:

#17, All garden beds are simplified.

#9, The painting for the kitchen, breakfast room, den, back hall are all scheduled TO BEGIN late fall.

#8, I have a buyer for the hot tub!

#13, The potting shed is completely cleaned and all extra supplies have been freecycled.

#16, All bushes and trees have been pruned.

For me, choosing to work outdoors in the good weather is critical to handle outdoor tasks, even if indoor ones get delayed. I could say I still needed to work inside, but the summer weather will be hotter and I will be able to accomplish inside whatever is on the list during the heat or rain.

What am I learning from this?

Even though it was 60 degrees this past week, it was 85 degrees above the garage and getting hotter. Smart to work on de-cluttering that area while I still was feeling energized. I realized that this area needs to be accomplished much earlier in the Spring season. So this will be next on my list.

What's Next:

1. De-cluttering the other half of the garage attic.
2. Cleaning out another cabinet in the living room.
3. Taking newer items to the consignment store.
4. Freecycling items that are up in the loft.

MAY 5, 2008
A BREATH OF FRESH AIR

LISTS OF GOALS COMPLETED TO DATE:

#s 1, 2, 3, 7, 8, 9, 13, 14, 15, 16, 17, 18, 21, 22, 26, 30

Over the past two weeks I have:

#14, The loft above the mudroom is completely sorted, reorganized and boxes labeled. All unwanted items were freecycled.

#18, Planted one-half of the vegetable garden, other half to be done in two weeks when the weather is a bit warmer.

#22, Completed going through every file in all the cabinets: shredded, simplified, combined.

#26, All living-room cabinets under the bookcase have been cleaned out and simplified.

#3, Took more to the consignment store.

What am I learning from this?

At first I was daunted by the amount of stuff in the loft. As we do not have an attic in the house or a full basement, items we want to keep protected end up there. Extra lampshades, pictures, small rugs, kids' pottery, sentimental childhood items and their personal ones, current paints, etc.

In my mind I sectioned off the space and did one-quarter of the area at a time. This made the space DOABLE and MEASURABLE. Remember the S.M.A.R.T goals: s-specific, simple; m-measurable; a-attainable; r-realistic; t-time oriented.

What's Next:

#7, Another batch to go to the consignment store tomorrow.

#25, Call the Town Hall and ask them what their policy is regarding environmentally recycling and disposing of paints.

JUNE 3, 2008

FEELING LIGHTER AND LIGHTER

LISTS OF GOALS COMPLETED TO DATE:

#s 1, 2, 3, 7, 8, 9, 12, 13, 14, 15, 16, 17, 18, 21, 22, 24, 26, 30

I have accomplished 18 out of my 30 goals total...not bad, half a year, another half to go!

What am I learning from this?

This past month was more than a bit chaotic. One of our sons was in an avalanche in Haines, Alaska. For the past three to four weeks he has been here recuperating with a repaired ACL and his brother and sister are visiting too. Unfortunately for him, I was walking through the den asking questions of whether or not he wanted "x,y,z," or did he want me to freecycle it.

We got a tremendous amount done, especially when it came to dealing with the garage. We put a couch in the corner of the garage, plopped Corey on top of it and brought items down from the attic one at a time. "Want it, need it, donate it?"

While Sarah was here she went down memory lane reading her old journals, parting with some letters, artwork and notes from grade-school classes. She could not believe she held on to some of it. Taylor wanted to hold on to almost nothing. His response; "Way too much to cart around."

This is cathartic.

What's Next:

#25, Need to call the Town Hall to ask about paint disposal policy

#5, 20, Start on closets and drawers.

WHEN ONE DOOR CLOSES ANOTHER ONE OPENS

LISTS OF GOALS COMPLETED TO DATE:

#s 1, 2, 3, 7, 9, 10, 12, 13, 14, 15, 16, 17, 18, 21, 22, 24, 25, 26, 28, 30

(19 out of 30...11 more to go!)

Have you ever noticed "when one door closes another one opens?" For example, after spending all this time de-cluttering, ridding my house of all the things that we no longer needed...my husband's parents' house sold and the furniture needed to be divided amongst the three grown siblings. (There was a moment of panic when I thought of all the furniture and other stuff that would now be descending upon us and into the house...after my six months of cleaning and clearing, ugh!). Here is where the door opened: Attitude change.

For years we had not used the living room because pieces of furniture were being moved from one place to another. It became the "storage" unit for my own family of origins... furniture, knick knacks, paintings, etc...until I finally decided what to do with it all. I must admit the living room was not a high priority on my list, as we never used it often enough. The thought of redecorating, covering and reupholster was daunting and costly. We lived in our den, which we always found to be cozier with roaring fires, especially in the cold winters.

When my husband came back from selecting what he might like from his parent's house, I was surprised to learn that much of what he selected would have been my choice too. And they all were living room furniture pieces!

Last night, we had his family over for dinner, we used the living room for the first time in four years! It gave them and us great pleasure to see where the furniture from their past was now living.

So just when you think you have cleared and cleaned out and have all your ducks in a row, don't be surprised if some other door opens. Greet it with enthusiasm and curiosity; you never know where it will take you. Lesson: be open to receive.

What's Next:

1. Move all "inherited" furniture to storage unit for kids' future houses or apartments.
2. Take painting to auction house for sale.
3. #5, Go through my closet on a rainy day this week.
4. #20, Go through all my drawers in my bedroom.
5. #5, Redo and reorganize linen closet.
6. #3, Take more to the consignment store.
7. #8, Hot tub fell through, so I need to try and sell it one more time.

JULY 20, 2008
ONE DRAWER AT A TIME

I am moving further still!

#3, Taking more tomorrow to the consignment store.

#20, Went through all my bureau drawers. How many short sleeve shirts does one person need?

What's Next:

#5, Tomorrow I believe it is going to rain...so I will hit Corey's closet and then tackle mine. When #5 is finished, the entire upstairs will have been done!!!

OCTOBER, 2008
HOME STRETCH

LIST OF GOALS COMPLETED TO DATE:

#s 1, 2, 3, 5, 7, 9, 10, 12, 13, 14, 15, 16, 17, 18, 19, 20, 21, 22, 23, 24, 25, 26, 27, 28, 30

(25 COMPLETED...5 TO GO!)

Can't believe that I last posted July 20!!!

I am sorry, the de-cluttering has taken on a life of its own and the accountability to share my progress got put aside.

What am I learning from this?

Even though I have not shared these past four months with you, I never gave up continuing to work away at this clutter. I kept myself always having the vision and the Finish Line in sight, what that would look like...the end result, the goal. This has been a long process, but if one takes chunks, breaks it down, it can be done!!! So go for it!

What's Next:

Five more left to do...whew...**and two of them are, of course, the ones I have been leaving to the last**...why? Because I really don't want to do them.

#4, Make a new website for the Rocking Horse with photos.

#6, Organize all the photographs from past *umpty ump* years, put into individual albums for each child.

(The pictures are already in albums, but this next step is removing each one and sorting per child)

#11, Will be done in the next three weeks.

#19, Stone wall will be fixed today.

#29, Look into different Yoga classes in the next two weeks.

So there you have it, the last five. Do I hear a drum roll? (I am my own orchestra here.)

Do I hear cheering in the background?? No, I hear the quiet conviction of setting a goal and following through, even when hitting the wall. It's those lessons learned of structuring a way for each job to get done...but it has to work for YOU.

DECEMBER 17, 2008

☺ I DID IT!

LIST OF GOALS COMPLETED TO DATE:

#s 1, 2, 3, 4, 5, 6, 7, 8, 9, 10, 11, 12, 13, 14, 15, 16, 17, 18, 19, 20, 21, 22, 23, 24, 25, 26, 27, 28, 29, 30

#4, The Rocking Horse website, has begun to gallop. Though it is a work in progress, it has been the focus for the past couple of weeks. Sometimes I thought I couldn't get this done, especially since I am not a techie, but persistence is one of my core strengths and values. I just don't give up easily!

Start where you stand and do one step at a time.

#6, Remember how I was leaving this step for last. Well, I have not procrastinated...I have taken all the kids' photo albums and got through three boxes (one for each). In the evenings, by the fire, while watching a movie, I have removed the best pictures and placed them into their respective boxes.

#11, I have asked my older sister Nina to help me with this task. And it is right up her alley, plus I love her taste! She is going to help me choose fabric for the furniture to be recovered in the living room AND I get to spend a couple of days with her one on one.

That's a win-win!!!

#19, Stone wall all repaired before the snow fell.

#29, Decided the hot yoga classes were just too hot for me, so I joined another exercise class. Feeling great!!!

What I learned from this experiment:

A year is a long time. Keeping up is a commitment. And the end result for me is feeling tremendously accomplished. No one said that this would be a walk in the park; and many times I believed I took on way too much. However, after three months into it, I had two choices: Continue or give up.

If I continued, I knew I was accountable to those of you who read my blog and listened to my radio show, "A Fresh Start" with Sallie Felton. To quit meant to not even *try* to succeed. I could have used any number of excuses to stop this de-cluttering project, but I would be cheating myself of several realizations:

1. What I learned about myself from achieving these goals
2. How to find a way to succeed when I'm struggling so the urge to quit doesn't take over
3. Most importantly, I never would have found out how setting and achieving these goals served me in the end

What I can say to you now, at the end of it, is that I grew from this experience and so can you. It is by no accident that I feel de-cluttered mentally, physically and emotionally. What it took to get here was making a plan. It also took passion, patience, strength, focus and accountability.

I leave you with this:

START WHERE YOU STAND.

Set small goals.

Be Specific, make them Measurable, Attainable, Realistic and Time-oriented.

Be kind to yourself.

Accept your struggles.

Take in the learning.

and

GIVE YOURSELF A CHANCE TO SUCCEED!

Chapter Two
Getting Started Tools: The Running Tape, Mental Clutter

"A quiet mind cureth all."

Robert Burton

TOOL #1

HOW TO TELL IF YOU HAVE MENTAL CLUTTER

*"In order to seek one's own direction,
one must simplify the mechanics of ordinary, everyday life."*

Plato

Read the following statements and make a note each time one applies to you.

- My mind never shuts off.
- My mental to-do list is a mile long.
- I can't let go of thinking, even when I put my head on the pillow at night.
- I often forget appointments, what I need at the grocery store or why I walked into the other room.
- I feel like I am having to do "everything."
- I frequently tolerate situations that are stressful.
- I feel unable to keep up.
- I feel pressured to be superhuman.
- I find myself procrastinating.
- I rarely say "no" to requests.
- I am always overdoing, over-scheduling and over-committing.
- I find myself doing things I don't want to out of fear or guilt.

Let me tell you a little about mental clutter. Often, it's the result of overdoing, over-scheduling and over-committing. We try to do too much in a day and the truth is, we sincerely believe we never actually do enough within this 24-hour time frame!

Mental clutter is that infamous "to-do" list that seems to be living in everyone's head - appointments, meetings, schedules, tasks and worries - and it looks like this:

1. What I didn't do
2. What I need to do
3. What else I should be doing

We all have these lists we keep in our heads that keep us up at night and make us crazy, but let's stop for a moment. Can you remember a time when you felt free of that clutter? Where were you and how did you feel? What did you do that allowed you to let that tension go? How were you able to do it?

Spend a few moments recalling what it felt like to let go of that tension and stress. Really let yourself access that memory with all parts of you. Recreating that feeling now—or whenever you need to—reinforces the belief that it's possible to experience that freedom again, no matter how overwhelmed you may feel in this moment.

My colleague, Tara Sheldon, a life coach and Feng Shui consultant, encourages us to look at the relationship between mental clutter and worry. She asks clients to look at it this way:

> *"Another contributor to mental clutter is constantly expecting the worst to happen. While one can argue you may be better prepared if something does not turn out the way you wish, doing so is not helpful, as well as a major drain on your well-being. In fact, if you are familiar with 'The Secret,' you know the energy you put in is what you get out – good or bad. You could be bringing the negative outcomes to you by focusing on it. Imagine putting that same amount of energy into believing and expecting a positive outcome! Even if things do not go exactly as you wish, having a positive outlook will make you better prepared for dealing with any mishaps."*

So the next time you find yourself cluttering your mind with worry, ask yourself what worst-case scenarios are taking up space in your head? How does it feel to imagine the best-case scenario instead?

TOOL #2

IDENTIFYING YOUR MENTAL CLUTTER

"Do not anticipate trouble or worry about what may never happen. Keep in the sunlight."

Benjamin Franklin

Whenever I do a workshop on clutter, I ask the participants to describe what mental clutter means to them. I am always amazed at how similar the answers are. Where do you see your clutter show up on this list?

- Worry
- Stress
- Fear
- Grief
- Obsession
- Anxiety
- Co-dependency
- Feeling "paralyzed"/stuck
- Ruminating
- To Do List
- Responsibilities
- TV
- Media
- Technology
- Things to Avoid
- Health
- Email/Telephone/Voicemail
- Commitments
- Schedules/Calendars
- Repetitive Thinking
- Deadlines
- Procrastination
- Prioritization
- Children
- Work
- Money
- Errands

Before you can get a handle on your mental clutter, you need to know where it's coming from. Below are some exercises I've developed to help you identify your particular issues and understand how they're affecting you. Take out your journal and a pad of paper and answer as accurately and honestly as you can.

Exercise: Creating Self-Awareness

Reflect on your day. What did you hear, read or experience that honestly, you couldn't care less about or had little meaning to you, but took up space in your life? Consider each of these items and how your day would have been different if they hadn't captured your attention.

Then ask yourself:

1. What does my mental clutter look like?
2. What effect does it have on me?
3. How much time did it steal from me?
4. What could I have done with that time if I hadn't lost it?

We are constantly bombarded with information from a variety of sources— social media, text messages, TV and radio, email, voicemail—that we often forget we have a choice about what we take in, how we respond and when.

Do this exercise for several days until you begin to see patterns emerge. Only when you see the patterns can you begin the process of clearing space in your mind.

Exercise: Taking Action to Reduce Mental Clutter

Now that you're starting to get a sense of what your mental clutter looks like, take the following steps:

1. Name three things you can do to cut down on mental clutter.
2. Pick one you can do in the next week.
3. Choose the day you'll focus on it.
4. Write it in your calendar so your well-being is on your to-do list!

Exercise: Be Curious

Mental clutter often obscures the view of what is actually working in our lives and what we're unable to make room for. Spend a few minutes with the following questions to discover what your mental clutter is keeping you from noticing in your day:

1. What was positive in your day?
2. What is something you heard or read today that was upbeat or inspiring?
3. Why did it touch you?
4. What makes you curious?
5. What do you do to make learning part of your everyday life?
6. When you want to energize the mind, what do you do?
7. When you want to quiet the mind, what do you do?

TOOL #3
LIST MAKING

"Knowing is not enough; we must apply. Willing is not enough; we must do."

Johann Wolfgang von Goethe

What does your to-do list look like? I mean that literally. Do you keep a day planner or are you one who has dozens of sticky notes posted around the house? One of my sisters uses sticky notes all the time to remind herself to do anything and everything—she even has them in her car!

No matter what your system is for tracking your to-dos, getting them out of your head and onto paper is key to reducing mental clutter. This is particularly helpful when you're dealing with a large-scale project.

I had a client, I'll call "Winnie." During one of our coaching sessions I asked her what was getting in her way and keeping her stuck. She said it was the mile-long list that ran through her head of everything she needed to do for her house, but even the idea of making a list was overwhelming.

Here's what I asked Winnie next:

Sallie: "If you knew you could not fail, how would that make you feel?"

Winnie: "I would be ecstatic!"

Sallie: "So feeling ecstatic, what might be one of the first things you could do to unload this list from your mind?"

Winnie: "I'd like to make a list - I am visual that way - but when the list gets too long, I start feeling like I'll never get it all done."

Sallie: "So, Winnie, let's change that sentence to be more positive and affirming. How about saying, 'I'd like to make a list and I will break it down into smaller lists in order to keep moving forward.' How does that sound?"

Winnie: "Wow, that sounds more doable!"

Why at first did it not seem possible for Winnie to make her projects list? The reason is simple: When you set a goal of writing a list of errands, projects or other tasks to complete and you've only completed a small portion of them, it's easy to feel disappointed or have a sense of failure even though your list is shorter for having done so.

And why is it that we do not give ourselves credit for the tasks we completed? Because we didn't complete the ENTIRE list and if something isn't finished in its entirety, we tend to believe we've failed. That, right there, is how we generate negative clutter in our minds. The truth is, we didn't fail—we just miscalculated the amount of time we really need to work through the list.

Now that Winnie was ready to take on making her list, we needed to find out what was going to be on it and how it would be organized. Winnie opted to name each project and call out what she would be responsible for, what her husband would do and what someone else might do.

The goal with Winnie was to get her to make the list and then have her systematically and realistically work her way through it. When you're stuck like Winnie was, it's critical to have a point of accountability. Winnie decided that she would update her list regularly to show what was completed and what was left to do, and email those updates to me.

Here is Winnie's complete list as of the last update. She calls it her "Honey-We-Do List". You can use a similar system* to make your own lists, but as long as you commit to whatever system you choose, you'll increase your chances of success and reduce the clutter in your mind at the same time.

 To download your own "Honey-We-Do" template, go to *www.SoSmartOnline.com/Clutter*

Project	Shane	Winnie	Other	Done
~~Refresh cedar in cedar closet~~		X		½ 9/8/08 ¼ 9/13/08 Done 2008
~~Get rid of dirt in garage~~			X	1/8/09
~~Energy audit (Called 9/3, waiting for call-back)~~			X	10/14/08
~~Chimney inspection and cleaning~~			X	10/25/08
~~Fireplace cracks inside~~	X			10/25/08
~~Replace fuel oil tank lock~~		X		10/7/08
~~Small desk for my BR (laptop)~~		X		11/1/08
~~Check that all bulbs are CF~~	X			11/30/08
~~Complete cleaning of kitchen~~ ~~Stove, oven, microwave~~ ~~Refrigerator~~ ~~Kitchen pantry~~ ~~Cabinet fronts (Cabinet Magic)~~ ~~Get rid of stuff I don't use~~ ~~Sharpen knives~~ ~~Organize under sink; move cleaning stuff to laundry room shelves~~		X		12/31/08
~~Move rest of my stuff from cat room~~		X		8/27/08
~~Move shoes to BR~~		X		8/27/08
~~Buy freezer~~		X		8/28/08
~~List to the 4 circuit boxes~~		X		8/29/08
~~Weeding and Preen~~		X		8/29/08
~~Cut binding on blanket~~		X		8/30/08
~~Install solar lights in side yard~~		X		9/1/08
~~Move china cabinet back~~	X	X		9/1/08
~~Move sofa table back~~	X	X		9/1/08

Project	Shane	Winnie	Other	Done
Set up my BR correctly, clothes and stuff (i.e., "move in")		X		9/1/08
Clean fireplace		X		9/10/08
Clean cobwebs in mechanical area, basement		X		9/13/08
Clean out junk drawers in kitchen		X		9/13/08
Clean up mold in my shower		X		9/13/08
Pest control outside (cob webs) (October)			X	9/13/08
Replace Shane's shower curtain liner		X		9/13/08
Dripping faucets (AAA Plumbing) My shower Guest bath sink			X	9/14/08
Organize shelves in laundry room Floors Laundry Kitchen cleaning supplies Bath cleaning supplies		X		9/27/08
Disposal cleaner		X		9/6/08
Finish filing systems Personal Universities		X		9/6/08
Fix garage door	X			9/6/08
Clean out credenza drawers		X		9/7/08
Clean out desk drawers		X		9/7/08
Phone in my BR		X		9/7/08
Repair drain under laundry sink			X	9/8/08
Birdfeeder		X		No
Get rid of ramp			X	No

What's running circles in your head? Use the following exercise to motivate and inspire you to take the first step.

Exercise: Unloading

At the end of 2007, I wanted to de-clutter my whole house, top to bottom and inside and out. Yes, this was a physical job, but it had been weighing on me mentally for a few years at that point and more so now that all of my children were grown and out of the house.

It was a lofty goal because the house is large, but I knew if I took the time to list everything I wanted to accomplish, then broke it down into seasonal tasks, I'd have a concrete plan of attack that seemed reasonable, doable and one that would increase the chances it would happen by the beginning of 2008.

Your mental clutter project needn't be as big as mine, but it should be something that's been nagging at you and sapping your energy. Think big and think outside the box. Don't let that inner critic tell you why you can't accomplish your goals. If you do, what's weighing on you now will grow heavier as time goes by. I know from what I speak.

Now, **make a list**. Use your journal, notebook or pad of paper and write down everything you can think of that you want to get out of your head. It's taking up valuable space in your brain. Putting this down on paper is the first step down the path of de-cluttering your mind.

Trust me, it's a tremendously empowering exercise, so be brave and let it all out! Soon you'll start to feel that each word you write is like pouring water out of a large bucket you've carried for miles uphill. The more you pour out, the lighter the bucket and the clearer your mind.

Finally, **chunk it out**. Break up larger tasks into smaller ones that are reasonable and doable, so that when you schedule time to complete them, you'll be successful instead of overwhelmed.

TOOL #4

THINGS TO DO RIGHT NOW

While list making is a powerful tool to clear your mind, there are other ways you can accomplish your de-cluttering goals, whether they be mental, emotional or physical. The good news is that they're all steps you can take right now to begin your own process. For some this will be easy; for others, it may prove difficult.

Open your mind. The first thing you can do - and for some, the most challenging - is be open to receive what the Universe has to offer. It sounds easy, but when you're feeling stuck, unproductive and find yourself procrastinating, it can be a tough hill to climb. You might feel unmotivated, frustrated, anxious or all three but whatever you're feeling, I can guarantee this: you will feel the weight of the mental as though it were physical weight.

Say the issue that's nagging at you is that if you were to actually clean and organize your desk, you'd lose critical files or information or won't be able to find it if necessary. You don't want to look at the clutter anymore, but you don't know what to do with it either.

Be open to finding solutions to help with the physical clutter and ease part of the stress. In this case, let's use a file cabinet. But wait. You don't have a file cabinet and now you're stressed about having to purchase one.

Really think about what you truly need, with intention, and be open to what comes back to you—a call from a friend who's moving and is giving furniture away, a Craigslist ad, an office-supply store closing sale you notice on your way to the market.

TOOL #5

MAKING TIME FOR WHAT YOU WANT

"We don't have eternity to realize our dreams, only the time we are here."

Susan Taylor

No one will come to your party if don't send an invitation to them. The same is true for anything you want to create in your life—clearer thinking, more balance, less stress, peaceful mornings, etc. Ask yourself:

What is it I want?

What do I need to support this and make it happen?

What do I need to do to quiet my "inner voice" in my mind?

When you have less mental clutter, you almost always feel like you have more time. Are you going to spend that time on yourself or use it to create more clutter by: watching violent movies; working on the computer until bedtime; mindlessly surfing the Internet; letting clothes, books, children's toys or other items pile up around the house; or worse, in your bedroom where you'll take it all to "sleep" with you?

Or will you make excuses like, "I don't have enough time to do what I want to do in the morning/after work/after the children go to bed." I'm going to let you in on a secret: Yes, you do. It's just a matter of changing the way you think about time.

Just like we experience feelings of failure when we don't complete our massive to-do lists in their entirety, we deprive ourselves of activities we enjoy because we're not able to sit and read that book cover-to-cover, go for a 10-mile run or start and finish a painting.

However you choose to use the space and time you've created for yourself, it's important you feel relaxed and give yourself permission to enjoy what you're doing in the time you have allowed.

As you've probably guessed, the same holds true when you look at your to-do list or a big project and wonder how on earth you'll ever get through it.

TOOL #6

HOW TO CLEAR YOUR CLUTTER

"Worry only about the things under your control, the things
that can be influenced and changed by your actions,
not about the things that are beyond
your capacity to direct or alter."

Charles E. Hummel

Limit your clearing sessions to anywhere from 15 minutes up to three hours, but no more. Why am I asking you to put a limit on it? <u>I want you to be successful here</u>. I don't want failure—<u>I want success</u>. A useful way to stick to this is to play your favorite music in the background. Usually, it takes 45 minutes to an hour for a CD to finish and you can commit to clearing until the CD is over.

Next, it is absolutely necessary to limit distractions. So, if you need to go to the bathroom, or you're hungry or thirsty, take care of it before you start. I also don't want you to look at your computer, answer your cell phone, your landline, the doorbell, check e-mail or anything else. And don't even try texting! When you're clearing, I want you to clear with no distractions at all.

When we release clutter in our minds, our emotional clutter tends to follow suit. We feel less stressed, less burdened and more at peace. This exercise is just the beginning, but done regularly, it has lasting results.

Make sure when you start your clearing process you have the right tools in place. What tools might those be you ask? If you're dealing with mental or emotional clutter, you might want a notepad and a pen to write (or your computer, with email and browser closed, please). Use colored markers and butcher paper if that's what feels right to you. It doesn't matter so long as you can keep the clutter flowing freely out of you.

The point is to get some paper and write down every thing that's lodged in your head. What's on your mental list? Get it out—all of it. Then choose one thing from that list that you can begin to work on right now and **Start Where You Stand**.

The following are some stories clients have shared with me over the years about the positive effects working some or all of these steps have had for them.

Client 1: Changing a Routine

This client has been experimenting with different ways of settling back into a routine when he returns from his many trips. As you read through it, pay special attention to how he tried one approach, and then modified it to fit his schedule.

"I'm having my morning coffee and checking emails. I thought I'd drop you a quick 'Saturday-morning hello.' I just wanted to thank you again for the clutter class last Thursday. I felt privileged to have your time for the entire hour!

I got back from San Diego on Tuesday night and before I did anything else, I unpacked my clothing bag and put my toiletries away while the cats were eating. In the morning I got up and spent 15 min sorting my souvenir carry-on so things didn't end up all over the place.

The rest of the week I have been doing 15 min after work and 15 min before bed. I've found that the 'first thing in the morning 15 min' is just not happening right now, as it takes a while to get my wits together.

I'm going to see how the 15 min after I get home and 15 min before bed routine works. Normally when I get home from work, it's feed the cats, put the kettle on, check the mail, check my email. I'm experimenting with feed the cats, put the kettle on, 15 min of de-clutter, THEN check the mail, check my email so I don't get wrapped up in something interesting then put off the de-clutter 15 min."

Client 2: Objects Aren't Feelings

I have always been a believer in re-gifting instead of keeping unwanted or unloved items hidden in the drawer or hiding it in a closet. I mean, what are they doing in there anyway except making us feel badly about them? Still, the urge to hold onto things for emotional reasons, whether or not we like or use those things, is strong.

This client was having difficulty separating sentiment from physical objects that were weighing her down on both levels. Notice how each scenario involves a piece of jewelry that no longer serves the individual and how she held onto these items just for the sake of it and the process I took her through to "let go" of the objects and release the emotional clutter.

> *"I feel badly if I give away something Aunt Susan gave me, but I just don't like the necklace and I know someone who would love it!"*

> *"This belonged to Joe, but I'm not with him anymore/we broke up...but we had some great memories."*

The reality is the client doesn't dislike aunt Susan. She is still her aunt and she loves her—it's the <u>necklace she doesn't like</u>. However, she knows there is another person who is perfect for the necklace...so what to do?

Does she allow the anxiety and guilt, which surfaces with mental clutter and emotional clutter, prevent her from passing it on which also adds to her physical clutter. Or, does she allow someone else to enjoy a piece of jewelry which he/she would treasure?

Release the guilt, let go of the necklace and guess what? Now you are de-cluttering. In the case of ex-boyfriend Joe, keep the memories and "let go" of the jewelry.

Client 3: Being Accountable

No matter what you're working through in your life or on your to-do list, it does matter that you hold yourself accountable to someone and report on your progress. Accountability plays a major role in changing habits, but it takes practice, patience and persistence to keep moving forward one step at a time.

Below is a progress report from a client who had several things to tackle while also getting ready for a trip abroad. You can use it as a model for tracking your own progress.

"Hi Sallie! I did my homework this weekend:

1. *Going through my photos*

2. *Selecting what I wanted up on the wall*

3. *Going to the store to pick out a matching frame*

4. *Mounting the photo*

5. *Measuring and trimming*

6. *Hanging*

I would like to get at least "Dali and the rhino" picture up within the next week or so to meet your challenge part-way. I am going to the UK on July 23 til August 4 to visit my friends, and my extra time is being spent getting myself prepared for my excursion! I was very productive this weekend toward my trip. I did the following:

1. *Made a UK "to do" list*

2. *Paid all my bills*

3. *Made a "shopping" list*

4. *Printed out my itinerary*

5. *Emailed family members my flight info*

6. *Called my credit cards to notify my travel*

7. *Shopped for my electricity adapter and purchased*

8. *HUNG DALI PICTURE!!!!!*

I'm VERY proud of myself to have done so much and not be keeping things to the LAST MINUTE as usual.

My goal is to have everything done (besides the packing itself) by the Monday before I go (I leave on that Wednesday). I have about 10 tasks to go! whoo hoo!

...what a productive weekend & day."

Can't you just hear this client's enthusiasm and excitement over accomplishing these tasks and making progress toward his goals? What would it feel like to see yourself moving down your own to-do list with feelings like this?

TOOL #7
DECIDE TO BEGIN

"The beginning is the most important part of the work."

Plato

Are you tired of carrying your mental clutter around with you, but worry you'll never be able to sort through it all? Or worse, do you feel like a failure because you haven't tried? Let's replace that negative thinking with a more positive mental attitude.

Decide that you've had ENOUGH and truly want to do something about the clutter in your life. Once you've decided, you've already started.

To decide is a choice—a positive one at that!

TOOL #8
LETTING GO

*"I am here to tell you, to promise you in fact, that simple,
tiny changes made one minute at a time,
one experience at a time,
will positively change your life and every outcome of every experience,
in powerful (though sometimes subtle) ways."*

Karen Casey

I want to share a personal story with you about the power of letting go. When I was in my mid-thirties, I ran a small cottage industry designing and manufacturing outerwear. As the sole designer, I was always working on a deadline. During this particular time, I was racing to complete the new fall line of children's vests for a show in New York and trying to balance it all with the needs of my three-year-old son and infant daughter. I was mentally and physically exhausted and mentally cluttered.

One night, I was nursing our daughter at the same time that I was sketching and my husband came into the workshop—it was 2am—and said, "Sallie, I know you love to do this, I know you do, and I'd never say you couldn't do it, but would you at least consider putting this on hold? You're exhausted. Are you really having fun with this?"

That was a major "AH-HA" moment for me! By having someone ask me to consider putting it on hold and <u>not</u> say you have to sell it or give it up was a kinder, gentler way of asking, "Where is YOUR life balance?" That made all the difference.

As it happened, I did put my outerwear business on hold and it wasn't so much "getting rid of" it, but knowing I could start it back up again if I wanted to (even in a different form). It was the act of letting go of the business, even though I loved it, which allowed me to be more present with my children without worrying about the next season's designs or upcoming deadline.

That for me was a turning point: It's when I began to say "**No**" to things that created more mental clutter instead of putting more wood on the pile.

Exercise: Practice Letting Go

Part of reducing mental clutter is letting go of what's not serving us in the moment (or ever). In your journal, answer the following questions:

1. What's one thing in your life you want to let go of this week, even if it's just for this week?
2. Choose the day you'll take action on it. For example, canceling the appointment, resigning from the committee, turning a negative thought into a positive affirmation, etc.
3. Write it in your calendar so your well-being is on your to-do list!

TOOL #9

HOW TO DEAL WITH BEING OVERWHELMED

> *"When we are the most overwhelmed, we are the least resourceful."*

Anthony Robbins

"Calgon, take me away!" If you are a boomer, you're probably familiar with this old television commercial. In it, a woman is stressed out by traffic, her boss, the baby and the dog. "That's IT," she cries, "Calgon, take me away!"

Been there? I have—**I'm there right now**.

I am struck, while writing this book, by how overwhelmed I feel at this present moment. I'm scanning documents, research and notes. Some material overlaps, some doesn't. At the same time, I'm trying to keep the project contained and move forward but all I'm really doing is making myself crazy and nervous at the same time.

As I'm writing this, I'm sitting in front of the fire watching each log burn from the bottom of the pile up and thinking that maybe that's precisely how I should be writing this book - from the bottom up - starting with the easiest tasks first. I could have easily changed the energy of this fire by pouring kerosene or lighter fluid on it, but as I watch this particular fire, I see that each flame has its own path to travel. And that's when I know how I'll continue on with this book.

In order for me to take a step forward, I have to take a step back. I have to leave the comfort of the fire and my laptop to come up with a better plan. I need to remove myself from the chaos in front of me, take some deep breaths and relax, then go outside to be with nature, which always calms me. In doing so, I'll gain the clarity I need to revise my plan, put distance between me and my monkey mind and be all the more productive for it.

Here's the plan I put in place:

- Chunk out the book documents and all material at hand.
- Keep notes on each chapter and put them in specific/separate files.
- Send important notes to my virtual assistant, just in case! (Yes, I have lost critical items in the past).
- Delete information that I will no longer use for this book.
- Continue to send drafts for editing to my virtual assistant.
- Continue to send the edited drafts to Maureen for reworking.
- Continue to deleted edited "finals."
- Keep only the final versions.
- Create Final Folder to hold all the final versions.

What benefits did I get from this?

- De-cluttering of the mind
- Organization of physical content
- A sense of relief
- A quieter mind
- A feeling of accomplishment
- Motivation to continue

Exercise: Crafting Your Plan

Write down an event or situation which overwhelmed you and explain why it did. Then answer the following questions:

What was your mind telling you while you were being challenged?
What inner messages were you given?
How did you respond to them?
And what did you say?
What steps did you take to get past the monkey mind (inner mind chatter)?
How did you remove yourself from the event or situation, or did you?
What action steps did you take to alleviate the matter?
What could you have done better?
Finally, what was your final outcome?
Most importantly, what did you learn about yourself?

> *"Amidst all the clutter, beyond all the obstacles,*
> *aside from all the static, are the goals set.*
> *Put your head down, do the best job possible,*
> *let the flak pass and*
> *work toward those goals."*

Donald Rumsfeld

Chapter Three
Practical Tools: All That "Stuff," Physical Clutter

"A house is a place to keep your stuff, while you go get more stuff, until you have so much stuff, you have to go get a bigger house."

George Carlin

Physical clutter is the one type of clutter we can easily recognize. It's all the things that pile up around your house, at your office—even in your car. It starts small, say with a few catalogs on the corner of your desk or the day's mail on the kitchen counter. Then, before you know it, it starts to grow until finally, you look around and wonder how you'll ever get organized.

Not only does physical clutter literally take up space in your house, car or office, it also has the potential to create mental stress. When it seems like you're on a never-ending search for items you need but can't find, frustration, irritation and/or that overwhelming feeling start to build.

The thing about physical clutter is, we all have it. We all have too much and we would all do better to simplify. But how? We learn to stay organized. And just like physical clutter can give rise to uncomfortable or negative feelings, you'll be amazed at the positive impact keeping your physical surroundings organized can have on other parts of your life.

TOOL #1
IDENTIFYING YOUR CLUTTER

"Have nothing in your house you do not know to be useful or believe to be beautiful."

William Morris

What does physical clutter mean to you? Do you have an area or areas in your house that seem to be a magnet for clutter? I call kitchen counters "magic magnets" for that very reason. They seem to attract handbags, backpacks, mail, magazines and newspapers, catalogs, etc. But one person's clutter isn't necessarily another's. Review the following list to see how - or where - your physical clutter shows up in your life.

- Attic
- Basement
- Bathroom
- Books
- Boxes
- Briefcase/handbag
- Car
- Closets
- Clothing/shoes
- Computer
- Counters
- Cosmetics
- Desk
- Electronics
- Email
- Extra furniture
- Files
- Garage
- Junk Drawer
- Kids' toys
- Kitchen
- Laundry/laundry room
- Magazines/catalogs
- Mail
- Office/home office
- Papers/paperwork
- Photographs
- Stuffed animals
- Sports equipment
- Voicemail

Exercise: Your Top Three

Take out your journal and, using the previous list as a reference, choose three areas where you have physical clutter. Then, assign a new page for each area you've chosen. Title the first page "Physical Clutter" and the first area you identified; the second page "Physical Clutter" and the second area you identified, etc.

Once identified, you are now going to rate it. Put a "value" on this space. For example, one being the worst (*severely cluttered*), two, three, four, five being the middle of the road (*needs attention*), six, seven, eight, nine and 10 being the best (*perfectly uncluttered*). This will be your roadmap as you move forward.

TOOL #2

SMALL DAILY ACTIONS

> *"Each morning sees some task begin, Each evening sees it close; Something attempted, something done, Has earned a night's repose."*

Henry Wadsworth Longfellow, from The Village Blacksmith

Physical clutter tends to collect when we stop performing what I call our Small Daily Actions (SDAs), like sorting the mail, hanging up our clothes, paying bills, responding to email, washing the dishes, wiping down the counters, etc. Whatever your SDAs are, ignoring them gives clutter a place to take root.

There are three key areas in our homes where performing our SDAs is most critical: the kitchen/dining area, the bedroom and your home office/workstation.

Kitchen/dining area. This is where we get our nourishment, do we not? Literally, in the form of the food we cook and eat, but also we also get emotional sustenance here by connecting with our families and guests with whom we share our meals.

Bedrooms. This is where we get our rest and when there is clutter in this room, it becomes more and more difficult to shut our minds off. Why? Because seeing the clutter in a room that's supposed to cue our bodies to rest stirs up chaos and anxiety. How can you possibly get a truly restful night's sleep when there's so much piled up on your bed, you have to make room to get in and go to sleep? Our bedrooms need to be peaceful sanctuaries. Period.

Home offices/workstations. This is where we need to bring focused attention to the work we do here. And for some of us, this is where we spend the majority of our time when we're home—especially if we work from home.

Exercise: Your SDAs

Spend a few minutes making a list of the small daily actions that need to happen in your kitchen/dining area, bedroom and home office. Keep the list short and sweet—your small daily actions should also be SIMPLE.

For example, if I don't take 10 minutes at the end of my day to tidy up the left and right-hand sides of my desk, I know when I return to it in the morning that I won't feel as focused as I need or want to be. I feel better when I start the day at a tidy desk because having physical clutter around affects my productivity.

It's also easier for me to quiet my mind when I stop working if I take a few minutes to make my to-do list for the following day and have it waiting for me on that tidy desk. I didn't always used to do this however, and I didn't establish the habit overnight either.

Still, there are days when I've been so busy, my desk seems to have a mind of its own. So much comes my way that needs immediate attention that it behooves me to stay on top of things. That's where my list of small (simple) daily actions comes into play.

My client "Christy," who works from home, shared how she fits her office SDAs into her day by breaking them up into 15-30 minute blocks of time. This not only made the task of completing the office chores more doable for her, but with holiday tasks like baking thrown into the mix, she found these shorter bursts of de-cluttering to be a delight.

> *"I actually use my office chores—de-cluttering, shredding, cleaning—as a break from my work. Holiday baking is also a great break. This morning, for example, I made muffins and streusel coffee cake, then cleaned the cat room (litter boxes, sweeping and vacuuming, cleaning food and water dishes) and did a load of laundry. Finally, I made breakfast and spent a little quality time with my husband before he had to go to work (Neither of us could sleep, so we were up about 1 a.m.) I took a short nap, then started work, made dinner, and did some more work. I have piles of paper, but they're sorted and ready to go. I file at the end of each day and take my emails upstairs with me to read and jot notes on before I go to sleep (and while watching TV). Before the lights go out, I have my 'morning piles' ready to go to the office and I can rest well, because I know what I'm doing tomorrow."*

"Ellie" wrote about her own accomplishments in keeping up with her filing:

"I am greatly relieved to report that I have uncovered at least the top layer in my 'archaeological dig' of the office, simply by taking the time to file papers into their respective folders. The rest won't be as easy, but I found some sense of accomplishment!"

TOOL #3

RECOGNIZING THE EFFECTS OF CLUTTER

"Simplicity is making the journey of this life with just baggage enough."

Author Unknown

If you really want to conquer your clutter, you have to face it head on by asking some powerful questions about yourself and your clutter. When I coach clients who are dealing with clutter, the first questions I ask them are:

- Where do you have physical clutter in your life? Name all areas/locations.

- What is it like to get up in the morning and see all your clutter? Explain how it affects you emotionally.

- Where do you feel your physical clutter? Many times the stress that physical clutter creates is held in the body, so think about where you feel yours.

- How is your physical clutter serving you? What's the benefit, purpose or payoff you get from it? (Hint: there is one, even if it's negative; otherwise you wouldn't have an issue with physical clutter.)

Getting answers to this series of questions helps us identify whether it's physical, mental or emotional clutter that's affecting our lives. Remember, the three forms of clutter are interrelated; it's rare we're ever just dealing with a need to de-clutter just one.

The last question I ask clients is, **"What's the most difficult part for you about clearing your clutter?"** Nine times out of 10, the response I hear is having to deal with all three forms of clutter and the triangular relationship they share.

But we have to start somewhere.

Exercise: Facing Your Clutter

Take out your journal and answer the questions above for yourself. It's important that you be as honest and specific as possible. No one else is going to read your list and certainly no one is going to be grading it. It's there only for you to do so you can get clear about what you want to remove from your life so you can make space for what you want to bring into it.

Now you know where to begin and where to focus your energy to begin moving in the right direction.

TOOL #4
DEFINING YOUR MISSION

> *"Reduce the complexity of life by eliminating the needless wants of life, and the labors of life reduce themselves."*

Edwin Way Teale

Whenever you are in the midst of de-cluttering, be it your office, your bedroom, the basement or the kitchen, you need to have a mission or intent behind what you're doing.

To help you get started, answer the following questions:

- What are you trying to create by de-cluttering?
- What is it you are trying to change or simplify?
- How will you feel when you achieve this?

Use your answers to these questions to craft your mission statement. For example:

"I am de-cluttering in order to live and work in a more organized space where I can easily locate what I need when I need it and simplify my workflow."

"I am de-cluttering in order to learn how to let go of the past, so that I can move more fully into the present."

"I am de-cluttering in order to increase the flow of positive energy and new opportunities into my life."

Once you know what your mission is and your compelling reason for embarking on this journey with your clutter, consider the following questions as you work through each area of your home:

- What's working for you in this room/area right now?
- What's not working in this room/area?
- What can you do right now to change one thing that's not working?
- What's important to each family member as it relates to this space?

These answers aren't set in stone and in fact may change as you go through your process. It helps to remain flexible, because sometimes our plans for a room don't yield the results we desire.

For example, years ago my husband and I removed our screened in porch to make a playroom for our three young children. The room had large sliding windows on three sides that opened up to the backyard with the remaining wall housing built-in bookcases with cabinets below to store toys and games. For all intents and purposes, the room was perfect except for one thing - it didn't feel cozy like other rooms in the house and it was far from the kitchen.

No matter what I tried to do to "make" this into a warmer area, my kids simply wouldn't spend time in the playroom. I created a great, functional space but it didn't turn out the way I'd planned.

Over time, the room served many other purposes: porch, dining room, storage area and now, it's my home office. I think I'm the lucky one because the view overlooks my gardens and yard which are a haven for nature. Probably, this room should have always been my office!

Another example of using a mission to direct the process of de-cluttering is my client "Anna." "Anna" was tired of the poor lighting in her living space and came up with a new concept of what might work for her. As you read through her email to me, notice how she goes through a thought process of what might work based on where she needs the better lighting in the long run—for more productivity!

"I'm so EXCITED about putting a worktable in the living room! I'm trying to decide on the lighting. I have a couple ideas. I don't need your input, I don't think. I think I can make do on my own. One idea is to put a floor lamp in the very corner,

that I can get from the thrift shop. And perhaps a swing-out desk-style lamp that gives extra brightness for certain tasks. Or I could buy a fixture that doesn't have to be installed by an electrician, but hangs on the wall with four or five light bulbs in a row that would give lots of light.

I can't WAIT to get that table in there!!! I'll be so much more productive in my crafts because I won't be sitting on the edge of the bed or kneeling next to the bed, with little to no lighting! Plus MAYBE I'll use the top surface to write out my bills once a week or write letters. Sounds good, right?"

Exercise: Make It Work

"Anna's" lack of a designated workspace with proper lighting had led to craft clutter in her bedroom that affected the handiwork she enjoyed doing. By making a few simple changes, she was able to develop a plan to create a new workspace for herself that's free of physical and mental clutter. Take out your journal and spend a few minutes answering the following questions:

- What space/room in your house isn't working for you?
- What's your vision for this space?
- How would you use it?
- What's not working now that's holding you back?
- What could work?

Now, read through your answers and identify one thing you can do right now to begin transforming that space into one that does work. Commit to the task by writing it down in your calendar and when it will be accomplished.

TOOL #5
DE-CLUTTERING STRATEGIES

> *"The more you have, the more you are occupied. The less you have, the more free you are."*
>
> **Mother Teresa**

Have you ever asked yourself why you need to hold onto all that clutter? I'm always struck by the 80/20 rule. If you're not familiar with it, it means that we tend to use 20 percent of our belongings 80 percent of the time. The same applies to the clothing we wear.

I can SO relate to this rule that I keep it in the back of my mind every time I begin to de-clutter. For example, when downsizing my wardrobe, I've started to become ruthless. How many pairs of pants do I really need? Same thing with the furniture I inherited—there are only so many end tables and lamps I can actually use.

So let's get started, beginning with the three key living areas we focused on when we were learning how to implement our SDAs. Then, we'll go through the house, room by room, with emphasis on those storage areas that attract clutter - attics, garages and basements. I may not cover every area that applies to you and your home, but by the end of this section you'll have a good sense of what to keep and what to let go.

As we go through this exercise, I want you to keep these three essential questions in mind that are critical to ask when you're clearing clutter:

- Do **I LOVE** it?
- Do **I NEED** it?
- Is it **USEFUL**?

If you can't answer "YES!" to any of these questions, out it goes!

It's also helpful, as you begin to apply these strategies to your own home, to get a sense of the following:

- What's working for us in this space now?
- What's not working?
- What can we do to change it?
- What's most important to each family member as it relates to this room?

Write these questions down on an index card and keep them close by— they're an essential part of the de-cluttering process and you'll be asked to refer to them as we move through strategies for each area of your house.

Key Areas: Kitchen/Dining Room, Bedroom, Home Office

Kitchen/Dining Room. Kitchens are the heart and soul of the home. It's where we get our nourishment and thus, is an area where we can settle in and refuel ourselves. Take a minute to think about your kitchen as it currently stands. Is it working for you?

 Visit www.SoSmartOnline.com/Clutter for a list of Practical Go-To-Storage Solutions

In order for your kitchen to work to its optimum level, your cupboards, lower cabinets and drawers must be organized. The first rule of thumb when you de-clutter your kitchen is that anything chipped, broken, rusted, burnt or is a duplicate goes out the door.

Problem: Your utensil drawer is filled to overflowing and items are jammed in wherever you can fit them.

Solution: Remove all the utensils from the drawer, wipe it clean, and put like items together. If you have two or three of one item, put the extras aside for donation or storage (e.g., if you have children who will be moving out soon, these duplicate items can help stock their first kitchen).

"Motherboard Mom" Jeanne Smith says, "Here's a smart way to figure out what you're really using. Toss everything—all the spatulas, rubber scrapers, pie servers, and so on—into a box. As you use a utensil from the box, put it back in the drawer. After a month, check what's left in the box. Keep those once-a-year items that remain in the box, like a turkey baster or candy thermometer. But donate the rest."

When I inherited the leftover kitchen utensils from my grandmother and my mother, I went through each box, sorted and placed liked items together. I discarded anything rusty, broken or was simply too worn.

Then, I went through some of my own kitchen utensils and decided I would rather have a new whisk or carving knife than the same one I had been using for 36 years. I brought three boxes into the kitchen and labeled each box with the name of one of my adult children. I divided the duplicate items among the kids so they'd each have their own kitchen box to do with as they wished.

After utensils, inventory your drinking glasses and coffee mugs. These items tend to multiply seemingly on their own, taking up major real estate in the cupboards. I don't know about you but I could open a tavern with the glassware we received as wedding presents, never mind the additions over the years.

Start by weeding out all the glasses you don't like and the mugs you never use. You'll be surprised by the collection you put together. Again, I divided these among my children, but you can also designate these for various charities as well.

Food storage containers are another item that can quickly take over your kitchen. The Golden Rule here is to match tops and bottoms. Anything without a mate gets recycled. I have a sister who places a number on the top of the lid and places the corresponding number to the bottom container. Ingenious!

Ditto all those flower vases you've amassed over the years from Valentine's Day, birthdays, anniversaries, etc. How many of them do you actually use? Pare your vases down to two or three and donate the rest. I posted an ad on freecycle.org for 12 vases I no longer wanted and someone came to pick them up in mere hours. I'd also tried bringing them to a florist, but amazingly, they said they only used new ones.

Next, what about all the food in your cabinets or pantry shelves? I seem to be a collector of salad dressings—at one time, my son counted 36 of them in the pantry and in the fridge. Okay, I got the point!

Problem: Too much salad dressing (or other food item). I'm probably not going to use all of them so what do I do?

Solution: Check the expiration dates on everything in your pantry, fridge and freezer. Compost or dispose of any expired items appropriately then recycle the container. What's not expired and you know you won't use can go to your local food pantry. If you can, restock the pantry by putting the items that will expire first, at the front of the shelves so you can use them before they go bad.

Dried herbs and spices can be particularly tricky. They don't grow mold or appear to go bad, but they do lose their flavor and potency over time. I learned this from one of my sisters who is a gourmet cook. She'll deny this description of her talents, but it's true.

Problem: Your spice cabinet is crammed full of bottles. How do you know what you have and whether it's still good?

Solution: McCormick and Schilling brand spices make it easy by providing an online tool that walks you through expiration dates and freshness checks. Go to: mccormick.com/Spices101/HowOldSpices.aspx.

If you have other spice brands (and we all do), six months is a good timeline to follow for freshness. Depending on how often you cook, consider purchasing spices in smaller quantities to minimize waste.

Like flies to fly paper, clutter to kitchen counters. If any area of my house could be Velcro®, this is it! My kitchen counters attract anything and everything. Countertops seem to be the dumping ground for a lot of households.

How do we keep the clutter at bay here? First, consider what you are putting on the counters and whether it needs to be there. Does the mail really need to be piling up on the corner? What about the school art projects and the homework papers? Where do these items really belong? Identify where they should go, and put them there.

Here are some ways a few of my clients have found solutions to their kitchen counter woes:

"Janet"

> *"I'm writing to let you know that I came up with a solution for the kitchen island that I think will work. I'm going to use my small kitchen desk rather than another using the clothes tree and getting another table. I'm in the process of looking for some nice containers and maybe even putting up a small shelf that will keep things orderly. The first step is to clean off the desk before we go on vacation week after next."*

"Susan"

> *"You may remember my mentioning that I've been looking for freestanding lightweight metal kitchen cabinets like the ones that were common in the 50s and 60s to organize the overflowing stuff in my tiny kitchen. Well, I put out another request for one on freecycle and I've received two!! One has two doors and the other is narrower with a hinge door. Plus, the givers delivered them to my porch when I told them I don't drive!! I couldn't thank them enough. I've covered up the minor scratches with magnets. I'm deeply grateful because the cabinets have made a major difference in organizing my kitchen stuff that needed the right home."*

"Ben"

> *"I've cleared off my kitchen counter and I can eat there, so I'm pleased with what I have accomplished. I also have a lot of stuff on my porch that is awaiting pickup by other freecyclers. I will clear the dining room table by the 15th, next Thursday. I'm on track with setting SMART goals - the deadline and accountability factors got me moving forward. Very gratefully continuing on my path..."*

Dining Room. How many of us walk in or through our dining rooms and dump book bags, school projects, odds and ends, purses, briefcases, bags of groceries, IPods and/or the mail anywhere we can? Next to kitchen counters, dining-room tables seem to be the next best holding tank for our stuff.

Why is it so hard for us to keep this area de-cluttered? Because all that surface space on a table just looks too inviting and makes it far too easy to deposit items there than to put them away.

So here is my challenge, what can you do differently today than you did yesterday to de-clutter this area? Could you put your briefcase in the front hall entrance way? Could the bags of groceries go into the kitchen and get unloaded before you did anything else? Could the book bags go directly into the children's rooms? Could the hockey or sports equipment go into the front hall closet, mudroom or in the basement?

What I am trying to have you do is to RETHINK the location of each item you are even daring to place onto the table.

It is also important to be honest about whether you use the dining room for its intended purpose or not. Would you and your family be better served if the room had a different function? A home office? Part of your existing kitchen? If I had my druthers, I would not have a large living room or a dining room. I like the informality of a larger den and kitchen area—gathering spots where people naturally wind up and congregate.

Below are some stories from clients who were working on their dining rooms:

"Lisa"

"The dining room table is clear except for a contained section where I keep my checkbook and bills/charity envelopes. I'm about to offer a few more things on www.freecycle.org and have several goals I could work on such as clearing papers/ magazines from my living-room area, bookcase clutter, paper clutter in the dining room. My secretary/computer desk area (in the dining room) is overrun with papers. I will be clearing paper/magazines, etc... off three chairs."

"Penny"

"I think I'll clear off the chairs first as this should not take me long - I'll give myself a week. Sometimes I think I should be pushing myself harder to get more done, but that usually backfires, so, I'll continue at the slower and somewhat sporadic pace. It really doesn't matter to me which area I work on as long as I make headway in that area."

"Catharine"

"Just a quick update, I have taken all the paper clutter off the chairs in the dining room but I haven't gone through the stuff. I left it all in a couple of boxes... that's my next goal to get done by the 26th. I have to say that it is a pleasure to see the chairs being used for seating and not as clutter holders...small things can make a huge difference."

Notice a similarity with the clients above? They were taking one step at a time: Small Daily Actions. There was no rush and no frustration as they applied the principles of defining the SMART goals system that you learned in Chapter 1.

Bedroom. As my colleague, Tara Sheldon, says:

> *"This is where our most private thoughts and dreams come to life. They are our space for rejuvenation and relaxation. When we have this room cluttered there is no room for breathing, there is no room for resting, our heads see chaos, and it feels chaotic. This could be described as both physical and mental clutter. That clutter also brings up the emotional part that is affecting us because it is all around us…in every nook and cranny in the bedroom. Seeing all this clutter around us adds to any anxiety we might be feeling about it. How could anyone possibly sleep well when one has to get the extra clothes off the bed in order to make room for them to lie down and sleep?"*

The bedroom is where we get our rest. This room needs to be our one peaceful sanctuary. So, what's necessary in your bedroom?

- Bed
- Bureau/dresser (one for each occupant)
- Closet(s)
- Mirror(s)
- Bedside tables
- Bedside table lamps
- One or two plants (great for your health)
- Wastebasket
- Chair

When trying to think about what is working for you or not consider:

- What storage containers: wicker, trunks, etc. might house your particular belongings?
- If you want to keep extra comforters and/or blankets at the end of your bed, easily available for those colder evenings?
- Whether wicker baskets are perfect to house scarves or belts?
- What area of the room do you read in?
- Whether there is ample light?
- If you need a table to place your catalogs, or magazines or books?

When I tackled our bedroom, I used SMART goals: One day I did my bureau, one drawer at a time, the next my bedside table, and the next my jewelry box. Did you notice that I did not touch my husband's area? Nope, he likes to have his just the way it is—a bit more cluttered than mine, but then again, I can choose to close his closet doors. I know he will get around to "unloading," as he puts it.

Problem: "Sam" was not the neatest creature of habit, his side of the room looked as if it could have been a locker room with socks, gym shorts and jerseys on the floor. The latest newspaper and sports magazines found their home on the scatter rug below his side of the bed. Then there was the exercise equipment. Did it have to be in the bedroom? his wife wondered.

Solution: "Sam's" wife might not be able to tame this sports fanatic by nagging at him to put away his clothes, but a solution may be to place a hamper nearer his bed or in the bathroom to catch each day's workout clothes. The equipment might find a better home in the basement along with his weights and bench press.

"Sam" and his wife came to a compromise—he now works out down in the basement, brings his clothes upstairs and puts them in the hamper in their bathroom. In return, she no longer nags him about the magazines and newspapers on the floor. Sometimes we need to pick our battles, and removing the exercise equipment from the bedroom was more important to her than "Sam's" reading material.

Home Office. If you work from home, your home office is your command center. It's where you earn your living, so staying organized is key to being productive. If you work outside the home, this may be the area where you sort the mail, pay the bills, answer email, do research, edit photos and write.

You may have an entire or partial room devoted to these functions, but the principles stay the same.

What do you physically need to have in this space?

- Desk/worktable
- Bookcase
- Office supplies
- Overhead lighting or lamp
- Locked file drawer
- Shredder
- Wastebasket
- File cabinet
- Chair
- Electronics: fax machine, telephone, copier, scanner, computer, etc…

Earlier, I shared with you how my husband and I had tried to convert an old porch into a playroom for our children, only to discover they wouldn't use it. So I asked myself what other purpose could this room serve?

The answer came when I decided that I would move out of a rental space downtown and have a home office. Okay, so where to start? With what I wanted to surround myself with and what view did I want to see outside my window? For me the answer was clear: my gardens.

Next came the practical questions:

- Where did I want to position my desk? Yes, facing the view!
- Where were the electrical outlets located, did any need to be moved or added?
- Where would the new phone line go in relation to my desk?
- What furniture did I need to have this space function properly?
- Where would my supplies go?
- How does this space suit my needs and does it bring me pleasure working in it?

As I began to answer the questions above, I looked around to see what I already had in the way of furniture to limit bringing new items into the house. In other words, what could I reuse and repurpose or make do with for the moment.

It turned out that the only things I needed to obtain for the space were a swivel chair for my desk, a locked filing cabinet (found on freecycle.org) and bookcases. It may not be the perfect looking executive suite, but it works for now.

The only issue with this space now is that behind my desk there is a regulation-size pool table! There is simply no other place in the house for this albatross, and though it was used actively when the kids lived at home, it's seldom used now.

Much to my embarrassment it is a superb "worktable" to spread out my documents, sort and file command center. However, the energy it holds is wrong for my office. I would prefer to use that area for a sitting area adorned with plants—a space where I could curl up and read articles, search the internet when not sitting "at attention" at my desk.

My game plan is to sell the pool table, refurbish two existing comfortable club chairs, slipcover an existing loveseat, add a coffee table and repot some plants from cuttings. DOABLE! What would that do for my spirits? Lift them up! As of June 2011, the pool table was donated to the community house and my game plan, vision has been completed!

Whenever you're de-cluttering a room or repurposing a room to serve you better, look around to see what you already have that meets your needs. Move furniture to other locations if the space is more suited for it. As we grow, our needs change. There is nothing that says you have to have the same furniture set up for life! Be creative…step out of your comfort zone.

Other Areas to Tackle

Entryways. It is said that your front door or entrance to it should be inviting. Why? It's the first thing you see when you get out of your car and the last when you leave for the day.

In order for this entrance to work, certain pieces need to be in place. For example: is there a closet; is it big enough; is it well lit; is there a shelf; is there a place to put boots and rain gear; and are there hooks? And where do you put your mail and car keys; do you need a small table?

Here is a list of items that should be kept in your front hall/entryway:

- Closet or coat rack
- Hangers for closet
- Hooks for jackets/coats
- Shelving or baskets for hats, gloves, scarves
- Reusable totes
- Umbrellas
- Outdoor shoes, garden boots, winter boots

- Dog leashes, "poop" bags
- Mirror
- Table
- Lamp
- Mail Sorter/basket/bucket
- Wastebasket and/or recycling bin

If, for example, your space is small, a coat rack works beautifully with a small table, lamp and mail bin/basket nearby. Remember to sort through your mail daily, recycle all you don't want or need to keep. *More on this later.*

What else might you need? For me, when children arrived, we needed a place for them to sit, put on and take off boots, dump backpacks and a reachable place to hang their coats.

I found that a bench worked well, placing small baskets under the bench housed their mittens and hats. I added lower hooks in the closet for them to access their coats and jackets.

Mudrooms. When my husband and I were adding on to our house, the most important area for our very active family was to include a very functional 7 by 9 foot mudroom directly off the entrance to the breezeway door. What did I consider to be a priority?

- An outside window for added light
- A large coat rod for hanging outerwear for a family of five
- Two upper shelves above the coat rod for added storage of sleeping bags and lighter paraphernalia
- Wall-to-wall cubbies for mittens, socks, scarves, garden supplies and gloves, household items, batteries, flashlights, cleaning supplies, pet supplies, etc.
- Four large, heavy-duty, wall-to-wall shelves to house our holiday decorations, miscellaneous fabrics, small boating supplies, sports equipment, etc.
- Tile or wood for easier care as flooring
- Space for vacuum cleaner, broom, bucket and small step stool
- Reachable coat hooks for small children put away their own coats and backpacks
- An interior door to shut off the room and contents

Bathrooms. The trick here is to make sure that everything you need is in close proximity to where it is needed. For example, the toilet paper should be stored under the sink nearest the toilet and not down the hall in a closet. That sure isn't convenient when you need it!

Essential bathroom items:

- Sink
- Toilet
- Wastebasket
- Lighting
- Towel Racks
- Mirror
- Vanity, possibly, especially in a larger bathroom
- Cabinet or small closet would be optimal but not critical for personal items

Here are some of the tricks that I have done. I have a mounted glass shelf over my sink, which limits the clutter. It keeps the clean look I want. All my bathroom supplies are in an old "antique gym locker" that I found at an antique store years ago. It was only last year that I really changed its function and brought it upstairs to the bathroom. We cut out the back part of the locker so it would fit into the corner. It has a very primitive look and works beautifully in our small bathroom. So think outside the box and reuse, recycle, refit, and refurbish.

Short on space? How about using a deep crown molding on the wall about two feet from the ceiling. This is such a simple and great way to store other smaller items.

How about using pieces of furniture to do double duty? If you have an old table or bureau, cut the center and place a sink bowl into it. Now you have a larger vanity surface.

Need more storage? If you have at least seven inches of unused/dead space between the wall and the tub or shower, add built-in shelves to accommodate both towels and toiletries.

Tip: Measure the width and height of the towels; that way they will JUST fit perfectly into the shelves.

Here are some things I have done to reuse, recycle and de-clutter my bathroom:

- Glass jars and containers store Q-Tips, soaps, cotton balls, and other small items
- Baskets hold rolled-up bath towels or magazines
- Unopened extra soaps, shampoos, lotions, etc.—especially travel sizes—are either packed into travel bags or donated to women's shelters or homeless centers

Medicine Cabinets. Do you find that your medicine cabinet is overflowing? No worries. Take everything out of the medicine cabinet, then:

- Check for expired prescription and over-the-counter drugs and bring them to your local pharmacist for proper disposal. Don't flush them or throw them in the trash.
- Discard any toiletries you are no longer using
- Group all First-Aid items together

Before restocking your cabinet, wipe each shelf clean—make it sparkle!—and you'll boost your spirits as you go along. Place like items together on the shelves for easy access. Do this at least once a year, more often if you can.

"Priscilla" was a client who was bound and determined to do some spring cleaning. The problem was she gets a bit distracted and has a hard time focusing on completing a single area. She writes:

"Today I have set the goal of cleaning out my bathroom with 5-10 years of expired drugs in a large, four-shelf cabinet! Everything is now on the floor, much thrown away, and I just have to put the remainder back. I would never have tackled the bathroom without you, Sallie. I am learning that to complete something I need to take baby steps!"

Clothes Closets. Each spring I am ruthless about clearing out my closet. It is one thing that I hate to have filled to exploding. How could I possibly buy another outfit and then jam it into the closet? I can't! So to make room for other newer clothes, some have to be donated or given to a consignment store.

For those who struggle with weight, it's tempting to keep entire wardrobes in different sizes, but all that does is overstuff our closets and remind us, every time we look at what's inside, that we're not at our ideal weight.

Donate or store any clothing in your closet that's not in your current size. That doesn't mean you're giving up on yourself or your health, but it will make you feel better when you open the closet door and everything you see fits well and is in good shape.

If I've lost weight, my general rule of thumb, is to donate all the "roomier" clothes immediately. If I've gained weight, all the "skinnier" clothes go to family members or are donated. Why have hangers full of unused clothes?

So very true! Here is my method of closet-cleaning "madness." I start by scheduling time on my calendar, either a full morning or a full afternoon, then use this approach:

I bring two to four large trash bags into the room along with two to three boxes. I lay a spare sheet on top of the bed and empty the closet in its ENTIRETY. Why do I use the bed? Because I have to get into it at night to sleep, so the job better get completed before bedtime! If it motivates you to have music playing, put it on—whatever keeps you focused on the task at hand.

Next, I group similar items together, making several piles on the bed. Finally, I ask those three essential questions about every item I touch:

- **Do I LOVE it?**
- **Do I NEED it?**
- **Is it USEFUL?**

If I can't answer "yes" to any of those questions, the item is designated to be discarded, donated or repurposed (e.g., old t-shirts make great cleaning rags). Other items ripe for the discard pile are anything that's permanently stained or torn beyond repair.

Be ruthless. If you tell me you wear everything in your closet, I won't believe you.

"Yes, yes, yes," I hear you saying, "but I bought this on sale and I know I will need it someday." I've heard this excuse and plenty more. Some of them have come out of my own mouth. When you stop and commit to be honest and realistic, you'll probably find that that great dress that you bought on sale still has the tags on it. You loved it so much you never wore it—are you getting the point?

Another trick I use is when I have gone through all my dresses, skirts, blouses etc., I hang them back in the closet, all facing the same way. Each time I wear an article of clothing, I replace it in the closet with the hanger facing the opposite way. Why? Soon I have a visual representation of what I actually wore and what hung in the closet, unused. The message for me can't be clearer! Yes, Cinderella, what if you were to go the ball…then save one formal dress, but not five!

And how many blue sweaters do you really need? Come on be honest. Black pants? Shoes? Jackets? The list goes on.

We all have a weakness for something and my weakness is shoes. I will try on a pair of shoes and, they fit nicely at the store, but later, when I wear them for a longer period of time I might find they're too tight, pinch my toes or just aren't as comfortable as I remembered. So, what do I do…put them back on the shelf hoping that they will miraculously emerge being more comfortable on my foot the next time around. Never happens—time to move on, Sallie, time to let someone else's foot have the pleasure of strutting in that pair of heels.

Some of my clients actually resist the idea of removing a majority of their clothes they NEVER wear by saying, "I NEED this!" and/or "I paid good money for it!" This is an example of the emotional clutter tipping its hat and saying "hello." These people simply need more time to sit with the concept that if they are not using it or it brings up bad feelings or memories then it's time to let go. Please, heal yourself in more ways than you think possible and pass on these items to someone who can truly use them and appreciate having them.

Problem: I have a sister who ended her corporate career, yet she hung on to the attire for years. It wasn't until she planned to renovate her bedroom and literally had to empty the closet that she decided to get to it.

Solution: She hired a woman to come to her house and together they went through this process of scaling down everything in her closet. For her, it made it easier to have another set of eyes and another voice saying, "When was the last time you wore it? It was in fashion 12 years ago, time to move it out." A trusted friend or family member can also help you with this.

Tip: Anytime you bring something into the house, take two things out! That goes for shoes too.

Linen Closets. I have to tell you this is my FAVORITE closet in the entire house to organize and de-clutter. Why? Because it gives me a visual sense of accomplishment.

"Most of us have way too many towels and sheets," says The Fly Lady. "Some people no longer even have beds that the sheets fit!" She recommends two sets of sheets per bed and keeping the extra set under the foot of the mattress or in a drawer in the bedroom to free up room in the linen closet."

Linen closets hold different things for different people, but look something like this:

- Towels (bath and beach)
- Sheets/pillowcases
- Mattress Pads
- Blankets
- Extra Bedding
- Extra pillows

When I attack this closet here are the first things I do:

- Remove the entire contents of the closet
- Lay them on the floor
- Sort them into like piles
- Discard, donate, recycle anything:
  - Stained
  - Torn beyond repair
  - Unused bedding
- Put aside all sheets to be donated
- Put aside all towels and pillowcases to go to animal shelter

When you have completed that take a look at your bare linen closet. Place the heavy blankets on the floor or bottom shelf of your closet. Then, label each remaining shelf with what items you'll place on them.

For example, one of my shelves houses my twin flat/fitted sheets, queen flat/fitted sheets, king flat/fitted sheets, stacked separately, according to size. Above that I have my pillowcases and mattress pads for the all the beds.

The next shelf up holds the towels, including extras for each bathroom and our beach towels. When you weed out the towels you're no longer using daily, remember they can be used to wash cars, protect furniture or used to pack delicate items. Otherwise, donate ones that are still in good condition but go unused, to animal shelters - same for your old sheets and pillowcases. The vets use them for bedding after surgery. It's a great way to recycle for a good cause.

Game Closets. If you have children who play games or you are a big game player yourself, how to organize and store these favorite pastimes can be a challenge. I prefer a closet, but a shelving system will do just as well. Just be sure you choose solid shelves as small game pieces that come loose will fall right through those heavy-duty wire shelves and get lost.

Clear plastic storage containers are your friend for holding packs of cards, crayons, and pencils. Label the container on all four sides; that way, no matter which way it is put back the label is clearly visible.

Here's how I organize our games:

Top Shelf: Adult board games such as chess, backgammon, poker chips, etc. Put elastic around each of the games and puzzles; that way, if the box becomes tattered, the chance of losing a piece is minimized.

Middle Shelf: Teenage board games such as Monopoly, Scrabble, etc.

Lower Shelf: Playing cards, younger children's board games and puzzles. Use shoeboxes and label the outside of the items contained in it…stamp pads, ink, blocks, etc.

Lowest shelf or closet floor: Toddler and preschooler games. If you're storing these items on the floor, consider plastic bins on wheels—little ones learn self-sufficiency and can actually wheel the wanted games in and out of the closet. Handled baskets also work, but take care not to load them so heavy they can't be easily toted around. Open bins and stackable baskets are some of the best containers, as small hands can easily reach in and take items in and out.

Storage carts are also great for crayons, paper, coloring books, etc. Again, if they are clear plastic, the child can see what they are choosing. Makes life easier, because if you want to have your toddler or preschooler be part of the putting-away process, they have to become part of the solution. Enlist their

 Visit www.SoSmartOnline.com/Clutter for a list of Practical Go-To-Storage Solutions

help in choosing bins - let them pick their favorite color and storage types. If they like what they choose, they're more likely to respond well to the idea of putting their games away when they're done playing.

Children's Rooms. I know we all wish there was a place for everything and everything in its place—truer de-cluttering words have never been spoken—but the reality is, it is difficult. Normally, a child's room has almost all of the floor or carpet covered with the products of their imagination.

Let's get to the basics. What do you really need in a child's room:

- Bed/crib/bassinet
- Changing table (infants)
- Chair
- Closets
- Desk/table
- Dresser/armoire
- Electronics*
- Electrical outlets/wiring
- Lighting
- Mirror
- Rocking chair (infants)
- Rug/carpeting
- Shelves/bookcases
- Toy chest
- Under-bed storage
- Windows

*for pre-teens and teens: computer, charging outlet, etc.

As always, the first things to ask yourself are:

- Is this room working for my child?
- What are his/her primary needs?
- Is this the area where they spend time playing?
- Is this the area where they do their studying?
- What are their special interests?

- Do they share a room with another sibling?
- Is there enough closet space?
- Is there a place to put their toys?
- Does the room allow them to get their own clothes out of drawers and closets?

Problem: "Heather's" daughter "Mary's" room was a disaster. Books everywhere, board games with missing pieces, toys no longer played with taking up space—you name it. The drawers were jammed full and her daughter could not hang up her own clothes in her closet. There was no order, total chaos.

Solution: I spoke with Heather over the phone and asked what her daughter's age was, what she liked to do and what she liked to play with. I asked Heather what her vision was as to how she would like to see this room and then asked Mary the same questions. They both agreed that Mom wanted it cleaner and Mary wanted more floor space to play. I then asked Heather to take a picture of the room and email the photo to me. It was clear they needed to organize!

So in order to have everything in its place, I asked if they would be willing to look at the room a bit differently in terms of placing items in order to acquire what they both envisioned. They agreed. Here is what they set out to do first:

- Go through bookcase and donate books to the library or pass them along
- Go through all her toys, donate all outgrown toys
- Go through her drawers and do the same
- Go through all her artwork

By going through this exercise, we got a clear idea of what Mary wanted to keep. Her toys were placed into a lovely wicker toy basket that they had picked out together and both of them had input on storage containers and baskets that fit their specific needs.

Heather added hooks in the closet at the right height so Mary could hang up a light jacket or hoodie. The bar in the closet was lowered so Mary could be responsible for hanging up her clothes each day by herself. Her shoes were neatly lined up along the back of the closet. Everything was now easily reachable for Mary. She gained a sense of increased independence and Heather could supervise the daily "clean-up" ritual if needed. Mary also gained that extra floor space she wanted to keep her creative play alive.

Exercise: Paring Down

Take these first steps in de-cluttering your child's room and get ready for new ideas and inspiration to strike:

- Remove any and all broken toys, including any your child has outgrown.
- Limit the number of new toys coming into the house and make a plan to remove older toys as new ones come in.
- Provide containers or baskets to store the smaller toys.
- Keep bookcases holding the books and not the toys.
- Use a tackle box to hold art, craft and drawing supplies.

Children's Clothes. The same process you used to de-clutter your own closet works for your children as well—even better, you can include your child in the process. When I guide my clients through these steps I sometimes hear, "My child wants to keep everything." Possibly, but you can find out what he or she would be willing to part with and I almost guarantee you will be surprised by their answers!

It's also worthwhile to teach them about all the organizations their clothes and toys can be donated to and involve them in the experience of making those donations. This is a learning opportunity for children with an impact that lasts a lifetime when they realize other people will enjoy using these items as much as they did.

Another tip comes from Michaela Freeman, a mom in Oklahoma City, Oklahoma. She keeps her children's clothes for one year after the end of each season just in case the next time around those items still fit. What doesn't fit is passed on to friends with young children. "How can you put a price on helping another person?" she asks. Michaela has benefited as well— friends with older kids pass clothes on to her youngsters.

Exercise: Weeding Out the Closet

Make a date with your child to sort through their closets and clothing and use these tips* to help ensure it's fun and productive for both of you.

1. Keep your date!
2. Make the time you spend doing this appropriate in length for the age of your child.

 For a list of Sallie's Clutter Tips, go to www.SoSmartOnline.com/Clutter

3. Remember, they're going to outgrow most of these clothes in a year, so don't let sentiment get in the way.

4. Laugh and tell stories as you go through the clothes. ("Remember when you wore...")

5. End the task with a small reward to celebrate a job well done. (E.g., going for ice cream, a later bedtime, an extra bedtime story.)

Children's Artwork. It goes without saying that your child's artwork is a masterpiece! However, that doesn't mean that you need to keep every single "canvas." Remember, you have the options of displaying it on the wall, saving it into an album or even taking a photo of it. In this day and age, what about a digital "art gallery." It takes up a lot less space!

With my own children, I'd start each year by putting a long, rectangular box under each child's bed. In it we stored all of their papers, artwork and "treasures" from that school year. When school was out for the year, I made a date with each of them to go through the contents of their box. They told stories of "making it" or "writing about it." It was a way of remembering the year. It was also a wonderful way for me to hear their stories.

Our goal was to lighten the clutter load *together*. When I explained that we just can't collect and keep every piece of paper we use, or draw, just as we can't collect all the mail, catalogs that enter the house...it made visual sense to them. Instead, I ASKED - by getting their permission! - which items they would like to use to do crafts with me, like making gift tags, holiday cards, wrapping paper, etc.

I also asked which ones were not their most favorite, and would they be willing to recycle those. This is extremely empowering for a child, not only to be part of the process, but to have a say in what they get to keep or let go.

Exercise: De-cluttering with Creativity

We want to hold onto to everything our kids make, but it's just not realistic without creating more clutter. That doesn't mean we have to throw everything into the recycling bin, however. You can repurpose your children's artwork by transforming them into:

- Gift tags for the holidays
- Holiday cards
- Thank-you notes
- Wrapping paper from larger drawings

- Framed artwork that becomes part of your décor
- Digital galleries

Including your child in this process is essential to success and the bonus is you're teaching them early how not to let clutter build up.

Toys. I started teaching our children early to donate the toys they're no longer using. This is especially true to de-clutter unused toys before the holidays or their birthdays. For you know newer toys or art supplies will be arriving.

Here are what some parents have taught their children regarding donating their toys:

- Donate to day care centers.
- Give to orphanages.
- Give them to their friends.
- Have a yard sale and donate sales to charity.

The hardest part with our children's room is getting them to take part in cleaning up. Asking each of my children to gather their own toys at the end of each day presented a challenge, even though they were each given a paper bag and directed to go around the house, gather their own toys and bring them to their rooms.

So I had to put a new system into place: If their toys weren't picked up by a certain time on a certain date, I gathered these "homeless" toys together and donated them. It about killed me to follow through, for there were birthday presents I had bought that I was now giving away! I had to let it go. If I did not follow through with my request, this would be a forever battle of "clean this up now, please!" The good news is, it took losing their toys *only once* for them to know I was serious.

I must admit though, that there are some very sentimental toys and books that I can imagine my grandchildren will play with, so yes, I have saved a few, stored them in a clear plastic storage bin labeled "For Grandchildren" that sits in the garage attic.

"Molly" wrote about what she did with her children:

> *"At the end of the day I had each of my kids take a bag and gather all their toys that were all over the house and return them to either the play room or their own room. It was great to involve them in the de-cluttering and taking responsibility for their own toys."*

Electronics. With the role that technology plays in our lives today, it's easy to get all tangled up in the clutter of computers, printers, scanners, digital cameras, mp3 players, headphones, cell phones, e-readers and the like, never mind all the power supplies, USB cables, chargers and extra batteries. The rate at which the newer, faster, shinier version of your electronics comes to market only adds to the mess.

The process of sorting through your electronics isn't much different than sorting through your closet. Start by:

- Gathering all of your electronics in one place, keeping the ones you use actively on one side and older, less-used devices on the other.

- Match all the cords you have to the proper device; place any extra cords in a separate pile for proper donation.

- Next, look at duplicate items and identify which items can be sold, donated or recycled and put them aside*

Organization tips:

- Use color-coded cord chasers/de-tanglers to keep cords tidy (you can find these at office supply stores) and keep things looking neat behind or beneath your desk.

- Store chargers in clear plastic Ziploc bags and label each bag with its contents (cell phone, mp3 player, camera, e-reader, etc.) so you always have the right charger or power supply at the ready.

Recycling tips:

- Donate older cell phones to women's shelters (check with your local library for a list of cell phone recycling programs).

- Check with your city or town to learn about proper recycling for electronic items (many cities and towns offer free e-waste collection days at designated sites).

- If you're donating or recycling an old computer, it's not enough just to delete your files—an experienced user could resurrect your data. Either remove and destroy the hard drive first or consult with a computer professional in your area to ensure your data is wiped clean.

 For a list of Sallie's Clutter Tips, go to www.SoSmartOnline.com/Clutter

Attics. Attics can take on lives of their own. Take a large surface area in a location that's out of sight, and thus, out of mind? Forget about it. Even the most organized among us aren't immune to its clutter-attracting powers.

Although it may not be practical to install cabinets or shelving in your attic, a viable solution for everyone is to store items in clearly labeled containers, garment bags or cedar trunks for clothing. It's important to remember that your attic will be the hottest area of your house, so you want to find storage solutions that protect your items from heat, dryness, humidity or dampness. Containers or bins that seal tightly are a MUST.

Garages and Basements. Great you have a garage! It's operational, but for some strange reason the car lives in the driveway instead, getting pelted by the wind, rain, snow, and the occasional overthrown baseball or basketball. If we were to open the garage door, what do you think we would see? You got it, wall-to-wall clutter!

Most of us use a garage for a dumping ground for everything. We've all seen this phenomenon or know someone whose garage fits this description. My own car has been parked outside from time to time—especially when the bay is full of items for freecyclers to pick up.

What we find in these spaces can be anything from 20-year-old maternity clothes to broken furniture, tools and sports equipment, holiday decorations and memorabilia. Maybe we have our grandparents' dining-room set or broken highball glasses that are still in a dilapidated cardboard box. When we look for something, we often can't find it because it's buried under other clutter, lawn equipment or tangled strings of Christmas lights.

Do you hear yourself saying this: "Oh, I might use it someday, or my kids will, so I guess I'll keep it." I've been there. I've also said or heard clients say things like "I haven't a clue where to put it;" "It won't fit into the house;" or "I'll just get around to that one later."

How do you get started with deciding what's essential to store in your garage from this jumbled mess? The most important thing to remember is to group similar items together into general categories. If you have a basement, the same rules will apply for organizing and sorting.

The most important first step is to open those garage doors on a day when you know it won't rain, grab the family and drag every item that is on the floor and walls to the driveway or lawn. Yes, I mean every item. Then once everything is out...sweep the entire area clean.

Take a step back and really look at the space you are now going to organize and all the new homes you'll create for that "stuff that you have." Go ahead, you can do this—and don't forget to breathe. I'll walk you through this step by step.

Here's my winning strategy for organizing this mish-mash:

- Spread tarps on the driveway or lawn.
- Place all items on them one by one.
- Have a couple of heavy-duty trash barrels nearby where you can discard any articles that are broken or unable to be repaired.
- Once all the items are on the tarps, sort by like items.

How to Group Your Items

Sports Equipment:

- Bikes
- Boating
- Camping gear
- Helmets
- Knee and elbow pads
- Racquets, gloves, hockey sticks, etc.
- Sports balls
- Skis and snowboards
- Surfboards

Lawn:

- Fertilizers, grass seed
- Gas cans
- Garden stakes
- Gardening tools
- Hoses
- Ladders
- Leaf blower
- Rakes
- Shovels
- Watering cans

Paints:
Paint cans are best stored in the basement or other space—not the garage. If your paint freezes, it won't be usable the following year.

- Brushes
- Drop cloths
- Liners
- Paint trays
- Rollers
- Stirrers

Garbage and Recycling Bins:
Label each bin with its appropriate contents

- Cardboard
- Catalogs/paper
- Garbage cans
- Glass
- Metal
- Newspaper
- Returnable bottles and aluminum cans
- Plastics

Tools and Hardware:
Keep frequently used tools in a lightweight toolbox that's easy to carry around the house for smaller repairs. Store nails, screws, nuts, etc., in clear glass jars or containers and label by size.

- Nails
- Screws/washers
- Tools
- Other hardware supplies

Holiday/Seasonal Items

- Beach/summer
- Fall decorations
- Spring decorations
- Winter/Holiday decorations

Automotive Items

- Antifreeze
- Car wax/polishes
- Cleaning cloths
- Container for spare parts
- Glass cleaner
- Ice scraper/snowbrush
- Oil
- Washer fluid

Pool Supplies:

Be sure to keep any and all chemicals in a locked cabinet or up on a high shelf, out of the reach of children and pets.

- Chemicals
- Covers
- Filters
- Hoses
- Pool toys
- Skimmers

Now you have a clear visual of the quantity of your items and the space in which you're going to organize them. Just like with all the other rooms in your house, you need to ask yourself:

- What's working in this space?
- What's not working?
- What changes can I make so the space does work?
- What's important to each family member in this space?

Next, take a piece of paper and pencil and draw a space plan of your garage or basement. Mark down where you'd like these groups of objects to be located. The goal is to create zones for each of these groups and organize the groups within the zones.

- Where do you need shelves?
- Where could a closet be placed?

- Where could some stacking bins go?
- What needs to be accessible all the time?
- What do you already have that you can use for shelving/storage?

Organizational Ideas

"Annie" was going to have her kitchen redone. It was winter and the carpenters were using her garage for their workspace. She had a brainstorm of an idea. She had the carpenters remove all her old kitchen cabinets and reinstall them in the garage. What a wonderful way to not only recycle cabinets, but to have shelves, drawers, and the needed space immediately available.

Here's another idea: What about a flat surface to work on in the garage/or basement? How about using an old counter top or getting an old door and cut it to the size you need? If you don't have an inexpensive door, go to a discount store or a home center. Make sure that you take the measurement of the width and length so it fits as closely as possible to the base you're using. Cabinets are good here too, but so are cinder blocks or saw horses.

Ask friends and family who are remodeling if you can take a look at what they're discarding or go to www.freecycle.org and ask if anyone in your area has some cabinets to donate. You would be amazed who might respond, especially if they knew you would pick them up yourself.

Having cabinet space in your garage or basement allows you to store things neatly and out of sight. Hardware supplies, for example: nails, screws, hammers, etc. This is a prime location to store bulk items in the cupboards until you need them. Go one step further and paint the drawer and cabinet fronts with "blackboard paint". Then, write what the content is with white chalk. It can be erased if your contents change. Or you can use painter's tape and a marker.

Pegboards. Pegboards are an invaluable tool for hanging lawn equipment, garden tools, or carpentry tools. It is best to organize these items by their function and keep those most frequently used at eye level and handy. Just make sure you get the heavier pegboard thickness and plenty of hooks. The nice thing about this is that the hooks can be shuffled around to different areas of the pegboard if space is a premium.

Tip: My father used to hang up all his tools on pegboards and then trace with a thick black magic marker around the item being hung. That way, whoever used the tool last would know exactly where to replace it. No more just throwing it in a corner, it now has its own designated spot. I learned this lesson well! Also, anyone who is helping you will never be yelling, "I can't find such and such…"

Garage and Basement Ceilings. Don't just use the walls and the floor of the garage or a high ceiling basement, look up! The ceiling, too, is useful and valuable "real estate" space for many garages and basements.

Add hooks for bikes, canoes, kayaks, or other larger sports equipment, like:

• Fishing gear	• Surf boards
• Skis	• Inflatables
• Water skis	• Camping equipment

There are also ceiling-mounted racks that are especially heavy duty and can take the weight for those exceedingly bulky coolers and camping equipment.

Wall Mounted Racks. Racks are especially useful if space is at a premium in a garage when you have a car that has to fit inside too. Because these rack systems are modular, they can be easily rearranged to fit as storage needs change.

Use them for:

- Ladders
- Wheelbarrows
- Hoses
- Beach chairs
- Rakes
- Lawn spreaders

Shelving. The use of shelves cannot be stressed enough. If shelving is what you need, measure the amount needed and do some research. There is much out there and if you go to a home center or discount store you will find a variety. Here are just a few of the types out there:

- Wire
- Mesh
- Metal
- Wood
- Plastic

Choose which one will work for your purposes. Keep in mind the weight of the objects that will be sitting on the shelf. You would hate to have the whole thing come crashing down.

My neighbor saw we were replacing all of our interior doors. He came over to ask if he could have them to put into his garage and basement for shelving. Another great way to recycle!

Tip: Square-sided containers make better use of shelf space than round edged containers.

Stacking Bins. Any type of bin can bring a sense of tidiness to a garage or basement. They create a real sense of order.

I had a client who was frustrated with the old dirty shoes that would track dirt into the front entry or kitchen. I suggested that he place stacking bins just near the interior wall of the garage side door. In it he put some clean shoes and slippers. The old dirty shoes had a cubby of their own and were to be left in the garage. Umbrellas, backpacks, flashlights and other things that might be in the way are also housed in these stacking bins.

TOOL #6
MANAGING MAIL, BOOKS AND MAGAZINES

"File, don't pile."

Sallie Felton

Gone are the days when the only mail we needed to sort through were the bills, letters and flyers that were delivered daily. Yes, there's still "snail mail" to deal with, but we also have email and voicemail to manage as well.

Keep in mind, the key word in organizing and staying on top of mail is habit. Taking these steps once or twice, or waiting until you're up to your ears in mail, is still just a waste of your time. Once these measures become habit, you're more than half way there. You will become a master of managing your mail and your time, more productively. Go for it!

Snail Mail. Everyone has their own system and habits when it comes to snail mail, but even the best of us can be consumed by this paper. Here is a typical scenario: We grab the mail, flip through anything interesting, check out the catalogs and magazines, avoid the bills and then drop "the pile." Where did you drop it? Was it on that front hall/entrance table, kitchen counter, dining room table, living room or how about in the office?

Avoiding the mail doesn't make it go away. Here are some mail management tips I've found to be effective:

Professional organizer Mary Pankiewicz recommends the "scan and stand" system.

"Standing is the trick," she says. "Don't be tempted to sit down. Bring in the mail. Leave your coat on. Find a place by the wastebasket, recycling bin, or shredder, and stand and handle each piece of mail. Put bills in a basket or pretty gift bag, take magazines to where you read them, scan any newsletters and bulletins for important information, and discard the rest. Your goal is to make the mail disappear."

Problem: Too much mail…too little time.

Solution:

- Don't spend a lot of valuable time opening "junk mail."
- When sorting, make sure you're near a trash can, recycling bin or shredder and toss anything that's not essential.
- Get in the habit of dealing with your mail at a set time each day, and keep to that schedule as much as possible.
- If you get behind processing old mail, consider using some "down time" during TV commercials to get ahead.
- Get off those mailing lists, stop telemarketers from calling you (I especially like being called at dinner time, don't you!) Go to www.donotcall.gov.
- Stop receiving credit and/or insurance offers, call 1-888-5-OPTOUT or go online to www.OptOutPreScreen.com

My client "George" was most pleased to email me about his recent success dealing with his snail mail and even came up with a system for when the bill was due:

"The biggest thing I have maintained is that I have been doing the 'no mail in the kitchen' rule as well as the 'open the bill, date it and put it in order of payment date' rule. I have also been maintaining my organization binder! These are now becoming habit and I don't have to even think about it or make myself, I just DO IT!!!"

Email. Just because it's virtual, doesn't mean it's not clutter. Your inbox is no different than that front table in the hall or kitchen counter when it comes to email. It's a magnet for unneeded messages, information and other correspondence.

Here are tips* to keep your inbox clean and stave off the overwhelming backlog of all that email:

- Make sure you schedule specific times during the day to check and process your email.

- If you can respond to a message in under a minute, do so.

- Delete any emails you don't need to keep immediately after reading.

- Set up folders for people or organizations from whom you regularly receive emails and file messages there immediately. Better yet, see if your email program can send messages to these folders automatically based on the email address.

- Create a folder called "Respond" to keep messages you need more time to respond to later.

- Unsubscribe from any mailing lists in which you're no longer interested.

- Important: Keep your e-mail address book up to date. File addresses individually and/or by group.

Voice Mail. First decision: where will you write down your messages? NOT ON SCRAPS OF PAPER! Try using a two-part telephone message pad found at any office supply store, or special sections of your calendar to record calls received while you're out of the office.

- Schedule specific times during the day to check and process your voice mail.

- Write messages down immediately, then delete.

- Save a minimum number of messages.

- Forward voice mail intended for others if your system allows you to, then delete if no longer needed.

 For a list of Sallie's Clutter Tips, go to www.SoSmartOnline.com/Clutter

Exercise: Making Mail Manageable

Write down:

1. What is not working with your current system?
2. What could you do to change it?
3. What new systems will you put into place?
4. When will you do it?

Books. Books are really difficult for people to de-clutter. Books are an aesthetic for some, hold memories for others—even those dog-chewed, worn out books hold emotional clutter for some.

My husband and I inherited a "wall" of leather bound books from my in-laws and they make quite a dramatic statement in the living room bookcases. They look neat and orderly.

Then, when it came time to clean out all the books in my parents' house, there were more than 33 boxes of books!!! As I took them off the shelf, I sorted them as I went: sailing books, garden books, cookbooks, navigational books, fiction, non-fiction, paperbacks, etc.

My advice is keep only those favorites. I have kept my childhood favorites in hopes to read to my grandchildren some day. Others, especially duplicates, give to a library...spread the wealth of knowledge...pass it on.

I explored selling some of the better leather bounds that my sisters and others did not want, but again, freecycle was my best friend. I posted a box of paperbacks, another of cookbooks, garden books, etc...when it came to the navigational and sailing books my curiosity was piquing. Who was going to want those?

I happened to be in the garage when an older man drove up, telling me he was the one who wanted that particular box. I asked him where they were going and he replied, "We have just finished building a replica of the vessel "Friendship" and the boat's library needs nautical books." How fitting for my father—lover of the sea and "captain" of his own ship—to have his books go to others with saltwater in their veins! For me, this was such a win-win scenario!

Tip: There were other books which I brought and placed into the large roadside bins of www.booksforsoldiers.com.

Magazines. If you are like this household, you have magazines inundating your mailbox. The first step in keeping these at bay is to cancel your subscription to the ones you no longer read. Be honest: if you have a year's worth of New Yorker's piled up that you haven't touched, are you really going to read them? I don't think so.

While I was in the midst of de-cluttering, I took all our National Geographic magazines and sports and health magazines to the art department at our local schools. They loved to have them for their students for collages and other art projects.

You can also donate magazines to doctors' offices, retirement homes, or adult day-care centers. I knew a former magazine editor who would say, "If you cannot read the whole magazine, do the flip-and-rip." She rips out recipes or articles she wants to keep and throws the rest into the recycling bin.

I had a client who was ready to de-clutter a stash of old magazines, only her husband was reluctant to part with them. After discussing the need to "let go" and make room for something else to come into their lives, he finally agreed that he really didn't need to hold onto several years of woodworking magazines. She was just going to recycle them with other paper goods, but then had the inspired idea to donate them to a trade school or college library.

Another client, "Rene", loved to read magazines, but never found the time, so they multiplied and piled in the corners of her apartment. Here is her solution:

> *"I'm taking my reading file to bed with me to get through some of the fun reading I've been wanting to do. I clip out articles I want to read but don't have the time and then take them with me when I know I'll have some waiting time. Why not go through them during commercials, too?"*

If you want to go all the way, stop accepting paper magazines into your house entirely. Most e-readers and many smartphones have applications that allow you to subscribe to and read magazines on these devices.

Exercise: Keeping Up with Your Reading

Write down:

1. What is not working with your books and magazines?
2. What could you do to change it?
3. What new tactics will you put into place?
4. When will you do it?

TOOL #7

CHALLENGES OF PHOTOGRAPHS

"Don't agonize, organize."

Florence Kennedy

Digital cameras can be daunting for some. Like any new piece of technology there are so many new features to learn. I used to buy the same digital camera as my daughter simply because her ease and knowledge of the device was far greater than mine. And if I had a problem, she would walk me through the steps to success.

As you know we can click away to our hearts content; however, your memory card will be quickly consumed. So what to do?

1. View and instantly delete bad shots.

2. Download only the good ones to your computer.

3. Organize your digital photos by event: birthday, vacation, winter, etc./and remember to label with date or year.

4. Share/email those favorites to friends/family.

5. Create your own webpage for easy sharing.

Our daughter Sarah was home for a month and with camera in hand, documented "A Day in the Life" of our last Alaskan Malamute Misty. Over 500 photos were taken within the month prior to her death. Having asked for copies, I knew I didn't want a pile of printed photos, and certainly not over 500!!!

Solution: Sarah burned the photos onto a CD for me. This was a win-win. No more printed photo clutter and I had the memories at my fingertips.

Once you have your digital camera, the question is what to do with your old traditional photo albums? There are two theories here: you can hold on to your old albums or scan the printed photos onto your computer and organize them digitally. Either way, Julie Morgenstern states in "Organizing from the Inside Out," "Either way the key is to make a decision so that you always know where to look for your photos—on your bookcase or online."

When clearing out our parents' traditional photo albums, I sent relevant pictures to my parents' friends, family members, etc. and kept those which were of my family and children. Only those that other sisters wanted were scanned or copied onto paper-printed photos.

TOOL #8

MAINTENANCE/KEEPING UP

*"Reduce the complexity of life by eliminating the needless wants of life,
and the labors of life reduce themselves."*

Edwin Way Teale

I cannot emphasize enough using the SMART goals and SDAs to keep you motivated to de-clutter. These are the pillars of the process. It is all about using your time and managing it correctly. So let's review:

SMART GOALS:

- SPECIFIC/SIMPLE
- MEASURABLE
- ATTAINABLE
- REALISTIC
- TIME ORIENTED

SDA GOALS:

- Small and simple actions we perform each day.
- Time to perform these actions is from five to 30 minutes.
- Actions that focus on maintaining the order we've created so we don't have to start from scratch again.

Here are some "keeping up" success stories from my clients and blog readers. It's my hope these stories motivate and inspire you to keep at it, day after day.

1. *"My goal is to get boxes ready for Big Brother/Big Sister. They take clothing and household items and as I start bagging and boxing I'm ready for them to go to the end of the driveway. They come pretty regularly. I feel good about these steps. I'm pretty disciplined so once I focus myself I move forward..."*

2. *"I had a list of stuff to get done today, but as my eyes were wandering, I noticed the bin on my desk and it finally hit me how much paper was in there. So... I decided to empty that bin of any paper. It was stacked about 2" high. I had promised myself not to fill it up or use it as a holding bin (like I used to use my printer; remember that?) Well, it's empty! There are a few sheets left of stuff I have to take care of tonight. The rest is put in its*

appropriate place and most got shredded after I read it. Cool!"

3. *"Oh yes... what I meant about "you're right!" is that I had the confidence to dig in, knowing I could get through it. Three of the items have a deadline for tomorrow (not a self-imposed deadline), to what I don't finish tonight I know I can hit first thing in the morning before I go to work."*

4. *"I didn't get as much done during the holidays as I had agreed too. Several unseen events occurred. I did de-clutter my bathroom and part of the kitchen. I did year-end and completed my taxes but did not have time to organize either office! I am trying to put systems into place for maintenance so that I won't keep getting into the same bind over and over. I remembered you talking about SDAs, and I will be more cognizant of using them."*

5. *"On the upside, I have received two rolling underbed storage bins* from a freecycler where I now store blankets and a comforter in. And the shredder I had found died, but I received another one from a freecycler. I have also kept up the now clearer entryway and more organized (and presentable) kitchen – and just offered about eight different things on freecycle and whatever doesn't get picked up is going to the VVF charity. So progress may be slower than I might like but I'm still moving forward. It's a process, but with the SMART goals and the SDAs I seem to be making progress..."*

Resources to unload the clutter:

- Tag sales/yard sales
- Donate to charity
- Throw it away, if unusable
- Goodwill
- Salvation Army, NO books or toys
- www.donatebooks.com
- www.gotbooks.com
- Girls and Boys Clubs
- Women's Shelters for cell phones, toiletries
- Homeless Shelters
- Libraries
- Church Fairs
- School Fairs
- Pre-schools for art supplies
- Day Care Centers

Visit www.SoSmartOnline.com/Clutter for a list of Practical Go-To-Storage Solutions

- Ebay
- www.freecycle.org
- Put it on the street with a "free" sign
- Return it to the original owner
- Return it to the store…if no receipt…get a credit
- Pass along to college students

TOOL #9
IS IT CLUTTER OR HOARDING?

"Clutter is a physical manifestation of fear that cripples our ability to grow."

H.G. Chissell

Have you noticed recently on TV programs and in the news the spotlight on hoarding? Dr. Phil had a guest by the name of John that had to move out of his three-bedroom home (so did his wife) into a small trailer because of the clutter he'd amassed. John thought his family was overreacting to his clutter—he was unable to see "through" it.

According to ABC News, there are "…at least 2 million people in the country with a condition known as compulsive hoarding. They suffer from a powerful urge to acquire and a paralyzing inability to discard." The story they did focused on a woman named Linda who was drowning in her "treasures" to the point where her disorder cost her a job and a fiancé."

And there are many more stories out there. Experts say compulsive hoarding affects people of all ages, occupations and socioeconomic levels. Many have even lost their homes only to have them condemned because of this problem.

Only once in my career have I come up against a compulsive hoarder. "Marsha" called me to ask if I could come to her one-bedroom apartment and help her de-clutter. She was articulate when she spoke as to what the problem was, "I have too much stuff and I just need some help sorting through it all."

We made an appointment for me to meet with "Marsha" at her apartment. "Marsha" said she would meet me at the front door when I arrived—and she did, with a smile. She was impeccably dressed and groomed but something began to seem strange to me when she whispered, "We want to be quiet as not to alarm any of my neighbors."

I wondered about this comment as we climbed the stairs. I certainly was not speaking loudly and she continued to whisper all the way up to her apartment. At the top of the stairs, she stopped, looked at me and said, "You are the only one I have allowed to come into my apartment, it is a bit cluttered and I can only open the door a little bit to squeeze through. I'm sorry."

What I saw inside was beyond anything I could have imagined. When we walked into the small living room, we were knee deep in clutter: bags and bags full of paper; stacks of books, fabric and clothes; unused electric appliances; canned foods stored in an entertainment center that was also adorned with dead flowers, plants and a rotten pumpkin; money scattered on the carpet; side tables thick with dust and a coffee table with week-old cat food and water bowl on top. Old chewing gum and rotting food was stuck to the parts of the carpet that were visible.

A narrow, but clear path about one-foot wide led from the living room into the bedroom and kitchen. "I need to make sure my kitty cat can easily walk through," she said.

There was no surface, anywhere in the house, that wasn't buried under at least a foot of clutter made up of anything and everything. Where Marsha had run out of room in the open areas, she'd tacked shopping bags to the walls to hold papers, articles and anything else she wanted to hold on to.

If a health inspector visited her kitchen, it would have been condemned instantly. Rotten food, clothing, art supplies and shopping bags covered the floor. She used her oven and refrigerator both for more storage. The sink, which no longer had working hot water, held a collection of plastic forks and spoons.

The back hall to the bathroom was the same as the kitchen, only "Marsha" asked that I not use the bathroom during my visit as she was embarrassed by its condition.

Her bedroom was particularly chaotic: her bedroom drawers held kitchen utensils, cans of food, cards and letters and various knick knacks. Clean clothes lay on the bed along with an ironing board, books, magazines and miscellaneous items. Her desk had collapsed, as had several shelves and bookcases, under the weight of her treasures. The closet door was broken off the hinges and bursting with gifts she intended to give and extra clothes.

"Where do you sleep?" I asked her.

"Marsha" whispered, "On the couch."

The more I talked with her the more I realized she needed professional help that was out my realm of professional expertise. This was not your average de-cluttering job.

We talked at length about how long it had gotten like this, her past, and her longing to have some peace and a sense of balance in her life. When I asked her what she wanted most, again, she whispered. "I want an uncluttered home."

Although I didn't have all the expertise "Marsha" needed, she was desperate to move forward, so I agreed to work with her for a month. After all, she'd taken that all-important first step by inviting me into her home.

What's more, despite the horrific view of her hoarding, I could still see through to her positive traits. She was creative and imaginative; her mind was always thinking of other possible uses for items and thus found it harder to discard. She also had a heart of gold, thinking always of others rather than herself. So it came as no secret that she would want to re-gift an item or several of them.

Our work together was slow and sometimes painful. Often, it would take an entire hour to sort through the contents of one shopping bag because "Marsha" had a need to read and evaluate each piece of paper inside of it. She'd then justify aloud why she needed to continue to hold onto it. Back in the bag it would go.

We went on for week like that. Even when we made progress like filling a garbage bag and putting it on the curb for trash collection, she would inevitably retrieve it before it was taken away, nervous and anxious that others would open it and see or read its contents.

Finally, I called a colleague of mine and asked her opinion on "Marsha's" behavior as things were not improving dramatically.

It was colleague's opinion, as well as my own, that under these circumstances, "Marsha" would benefit greatly from medical treatment and that unless she was seeking additional help, our work together wouldn't be productive. I broached the subject with "Marsha" and, after speaking at length, she agreed to seek medical psychiatric treatment through Boston University and take part in a heavily-supervised treatment program for compulsive hoarders.

Her first update to me said:

"I am almost finished with the study regarding compulsive hoarding, through Boston University. I am signed up to take the treatment sessions starting in June!

I am also getting assistance from Elder Services regarding general housekeeping as well as hoarding tendencies. Additionally I have a friend who has agreed to spend many sessions with me and will ultimately help me with utilizing my space and adding a few decorating flourishes!!

It's a long, hard, on-going project to change my habits and my ways, but in a few months or so, I expect to see a big difference. You can expect an invitation to my newly, permanently changed, habitable, surroundings."

"My life was so out of control, in every aspect, that I was getting critically ill from it. I was so overwhelmed that it affected my whole being...every single day. All kinds of things suffered as result...my relationships, my personality, my interaction with people, my friendships, my performance at work to name a few.

The clutter kept getting worse and worse, then when I was drowning so deep I finally had to do something about it. My health and breathing problems physically prevented me from being able to work through it!

It was so bad that I almost died at home at least twice due to lack of oxygen in my lungs and heart...because I refused to have anyone come into my home—friend, neighbor, EMT, or a stranger. I refused to let them see the entrance to my apartment, never mind all that it held.

I refused to go to the hospital for fear they would KEEP me and someone would see my apartment because they would have to take care of my pets.

It had gotten totally inhabitable and I knew the fire department would even have a fit if they ever needed to enter my living area. There was nowhere to step, no open areas, no clear hallways, and stuff everywhere.

The embarrassment and horribleness of it all weighed me down to the point it was intolerable: living in such chaos and turmoil was physically and psychologically exhausting, beyond belief.

In addition, I suffered severe financial problems due to not keeping jobs due to poor concentration (I wonder why) and being worn out (feeling like my home was a second and third, and fourth job) Just wading through things and trying to find things daily in order to function (function at a minimal existence, by the way).

Also, I was in a mess paper-wise and as a result suffered poor money management plus some depression kicked in. I was in a bad a mess as anyone could possibly imagine. I was in hell and couldn't find my way out.

It was literally a matter of life and death to make some improvements to change my life. The stress was killing me and gave me dangerously high blood pressure and worsened my breathing as I was always anxious and feeling charged up and out of control.

It was like living in an attic with the surroundings of a warehouse with out of control inventory and messes. I was literally wading through my belongings. The number of piles and heaps, for instance in my kitchen, were literally blocking me from using my appliances. I had to step one and a half feet back away from the counter because of the piles on the floor and had to lean forward, hurting my back, just to try and put something on the unclear counter. I could not use my refrigerator except for a bottle of milk and obviously my kitchen was in no shape to prepare meals.

Everything, I mean everything was literally piled up. Never mind what the bedroom and living-rooms closets and bathroom looked like.

The minute I met Sallie, I knew that I would love her. What an absolute delight she is. She has a very forgiving nature and puts one at ease in a very wonderful way. Anybody else would have been shocked and baffled by what a mess they walked into but she just jumped right in, asked me the right questions and quickly rolled up her sleeves and plunged right in! She is an absolute saint. Sallie had to enter through my apartment door on her first several visits SIDEWAYS, squeezing literally through the doorway, elbows tucked in close to the body because my door was so blocked it would only open about 10 inches.

I truly think that if I had gone on much longer, I would have stayed in my house become critically ill and would have died of emphysema because of refusing to let a relative into my living quarters or would have died from something triggered by the stress or heart attack.

Sallie has truly saved my life and thanks to her, I am starting to break through some areas, enjoy some small clean areas and know that there is hope. I know that this disorganization problem and clutter has been deadly for me and I am grateful that I somehow managed to live through it and am working through it.

Thanks, many thanks, Sallie, and I with continued sessions and encouragement, I know that I will be able to breathe again (both literally and figuratively speaking) very soon!"

I continued to check in with "Marsha" as she moved through this long healing process and was astonished, some years later to learn the house she was living in was destroyed by a fire. She has since moved into a new apartment with her cat. When we last spoke, I asked her how she was doing. The physical and emotional loss has been overwhelming for her. I sensed she had regressed...having lost everything, she may have had an even harder time letting go.

Compulsive hoarding is a problem of excessive clutter in one's home, usually associated with severe difficulty discarding items and/or acquiring an excessive number of items that one does not actually need. "People who hoard are often misunderstood. The general public thinks these people are just slobs or lazy, but actually most of the time it's because...of not wanting to waste things, and so, wanting to make the right decision about a thing that it becomes overwhelming and they keep it," says Jason Elias, a behavior therapist at McLean Hospital's Obsessive Compulsive Disorders Institute in Belmont, Massachusetts.

Pathological hoarding is far more than just mere messiness or keeping anything and everything. Hoarders can lose an entire room to the physical clutter they believe to be their treasures. Those who don't understand the condition would describe the same room as full of trash. Dr. Gail Steketee, interim dean of the Boston University School of Social Work believes, "They may have some depression, some anxiety, but mostly they're attached to their things in ways that make it very difficult to get rid of them."

Because it is compulsive, most often hoarding is considered a symptom of obsessive-compulsive disorder, OCD – an illness in which people cannot stop certain thoughts and behaviors. It is believed that one-quarter of those who have OCD could also be hoarders.

If you know of a compulsive hoarder, lend a hand and give them resources to get help.

*"When you have cleared all of your clutter,
you can be of greater service to those around you."*

Michael B. Kitson

Chapter Four
Feeling Tools: Straight From The Heart, Emotional Clutter

"Just remember, you can do anything you set your mind to, but it takes action, perseverance, and facing your fears."

Gillian Anderson

The following tools I've developed for dealing with emotional clutter are drawn from client stories as well as my own personal experience. These tools will address specific types of emotional clutter and how to deal with them. At the end of the chapter, I'll lead you through the five steps that will help you begin your own process of emotional de-cluttering.

TOOL #1

HOW TO TELL IF YOU HAVE EMOTIONAL CLUTTER

"All emotions are pure which gather you and lift you up; that emotion is impure which seizes only one side of your being and so distorts you."

Rainer Maria Rilke

Emotional clutter is by far the hardest type of all the clutters to deal with. While it has many of the same characteristics as mental clutter, emotional clutter seems to weigh heavier on the heart.

I believe emotional clutter lives in the center of the heart.

Have you been feeling overwhelmed, worried, anxious or resentful? Are you afraid of change? What brought you to this place? Where did these feelings originate from? This is what emotional clutter (of the heart) can look and feel like. This clutter comes from a deep place within you and plays a powerful role in both your health and well-being because, like all clutter, emotional clutter weighs us down, makes us feel trapped, overwhelms and exhausts us. It also robs us of our sense of self and authenticity.

Emotional clutter is made up of things like holding onto past hurts; unresolved issues, or past, present and/or future experiences; judgments; expectations; perfectionism and unhealed conflicts.

For example:

- The need to forgive a family member, friend or co-worker
- The need to apologize for your own wrongdoing and ask for forgiveness
- The need to discuss an important or sensitive issue with a loved one, boss or colleague
- The need to confront someone

Emotional clutter also includes feelings or issues we haven't processed, worked through, nurtured or released. It is the fear of the unknown and the fear of the future. When you're dealing with emotional clutter you may feel over-stressed, over-burdened or a sense of imbalance. At work, you may feel less productive, less efficient and less effective. In your personal relationships you may experience feelings of unworthiness, being undervalued, neglected or emotionally wounded or abused.

TOOL #2
IDENTIFYING YOUR EMOTIONAL CLUTTER

"Coming to terms with the parts of a change that you cannot control is critical to being successful. The most constructive thing you can do with No Control factors during change is: 1. Recognize they exist, 2. See them for what they're worth, 3. Let them go."

Chris Clarke-Epstein

Emotional clutter takes many forms, but when we take time to think about how it shows up in our lives, the labels we put on it are universal and easily recognized by all. Where do you see your clutter showing up on this list?

- Anger
- Unforgiveness
- Frustration
- Regret
- Grudges
- Guilt
- Hurt

- Resentment
- Illness
- Jealousy/envy
- Negativity
- Intolerance
- Remorse
- Judgment
- Worry
- Anxiety
- Expectations
- Inability to let go
- Grief
- Addiction
- Complacency
- Indecision
- Sadness/depression
- Fear (of anything)
- Shame
- Perfectionism
- Insecurity
- Self-criticism

TOOL #3

HOW TO LET GO SO YOU CAN MOVE ON

"When good people have a falling out, only one of them may be at fault at first; but if the strife continues long, usually both become guilty."

Thomas Fuller

Have you ever wanted to rekindle a relationship that slipped by the wayside? Was your voice not heard? How did it weigh on your heart?

Many of my childhood friendships carried through to my adulthood, but this situation with a long-cherished friend blindsided me. I'd felt the distance between us grow over for a few year's time—our lives had simply gone in different directions and we had drifted apart.

My friend divorced, then remarried and I was caring for my husband, who was dealing with deep depression and had also recently retired. Even though my friend and I had grown apart, I wanted to continue our friendship and bring the laughter we shared back into my life—our friendship connected me to my past.

So how could I begin to rid my heart of this emotional clutter? I picked up a pen and began to write about how much I valued our friendship, what it meant to me and accepted total responsibility for what I had done (whatever that was) that contributed to the distance between us. Was there a way we could reconnect, I wanted to know, and what had I done to bring about my friend's apparent decision to end our friendship? I was completely perplexed by the situation and needed an explanation to help me understand.

I received a very nice letter back—more formal than intimate—but my friend didn't clearly state the reason why our friendship ended. I wrote another letter to thank her for allowing me to express my feelings, but still didn't receive the answers I felt I needed. When we crossed paths at events we both attended, I'd make the first move to connect with her, yet her response remained cool at best.

Then, I made the ultimate "faux pas," I reached out to her on Facebook. Her response to my "friend request" was this:

"You've made this friend request in the past and I did not respond. I had hoped that that would be sufficient. That said, I am not comfortable being added to your friends list. I have purposely kept my friends list quite small—I only got on Facebook to stay in closer touch with my husband and my kids. Gradually, some dear and trusted friends have come onboard. I am amazed that there are even 30 on my list, as I have no need or desire to have more. I don't feel the need to get specific here as to why I am not agreeing to your request. Please just accept this as a respectful decline, but I want to continue a cordial relationship when we do see one another at events."

When I read this, my heart broke. I wrote back to her and explained that I'd been trying to mend our fences, but understood now that her intention was only to be cordial when we ran into each other. I asked her to please accept my heartfelt apologies for what actions I might have taken that hurt her and/ or others in her life.

A tremendous amount of emotion arose in me: the feeling of rejection (Was I worthy of being a good friend?); guilt (What did I do?); shame (I must have done something terrible!), and blame (It must have been my entire fault).

I wasn't angry, but I was incredibly hurt and my self-confidence was shattered. Now, I was taking the entire situation personally, which led to self-critical thoughts - whether I was such a rotten person and did I not deserve friendship - for I must have done something quite unforgivable for my former friend not to want to go into detail.

Do you see where my mind was racing to? Even though I had not a clue as to what the anger/breakup was about, I blamed myself totally! And for all I know, there may have been nothing I had done, but the friendship was being hindered by other issues entirely…out of my control.

What was I supposed to do now?

I needed to let it go! That was easier said than done. There were days when I ruminated about the letters, notes back and forth. It would have been so much easier if I knew what part I had played in this, but I didn't and still don't.

I kept saying to myself, "Sallie, you have done all you can do. You were clear in how you felt, what you wanted and took responsibility for whatever it is you did. IT IS TIME TO MOVE ON." And it has been hard. Hard because of the old ties, memories and the connection to my history. But, if it is the one thing I have learned over these years it's this: **You can't change anyone**.

I believe it is important for everyone to know they are not alone with emotional clutter. Below is an email I received from a client called "Betty." She has spent the last couple of years trying to build a relationship with her sisters after a blow out. Betty filled herself with guilt knowing her sisters may not accept her kind invitation to spend Christmas with her and her family, but she took the risk anyway and ask them to come. Here is what she wrote:

> *"This year's holidays will be simplified, to a certain, sad extent, since both of my sisters have opted not to come down to celebrate. I was saddened by the news, but was not surprised; since last year's tyrannical explosive outbursts on their part left me deeply shaken. (It has taken almost a year to forgive them!) I called them on Thanksgiving and at least we had civil conversations. Well, it does simplify matters!"*

As you can see, Betty was saddened by their reply, but knew intuitively she would be met with a "NO." However, now that her sisters had made their decision, Betty could settle in and make choices for how she and her family would celebrate the holidays together. By and large, what Betty wanted to achieve by clearing this emotional clutter was, at a minimum, to be able to hold civil conversations with her sisters.

There will always be times in our lives when we will disagree; however, if we can agree to disagree and move on, it's a productive outcome that serves everyone involved.

TOOL #4

TRANSFORMING BAD FEELINGS

"I believe that the very purpose of life is to be happy. From the very core of our being, we desire contentment. In my own limited experience I have found that the more we care for the happiness of others, the greater is our own sense of well-being."

Dalai Lama

A client I'll call "Helen" telephoned me one afternoon. She sounded frustrated and was feeling badly that she could not muster the courage to let go of her overflowing boxes and piles of fabric in her workroom.

"Sallie," she said, "I have run into a problem with being able to LET GO of all the boxes of sorted 'STUFF.' I still have lots of fabric, too—much more than I thought—even after all of the boxes I gave away. I keep going downstairs to the workroom, looking at and moving things around, but I'm not getting rid of it. I feel bad (guilty) that I have it and haven't fully used it with the idea that someday when I am happier, I will. And I was on such a great roll with this project, but now I'm feeling angry. I know it's holding me back, but I guess where I get caught up is thinking 'holding me back from WHAT?' I think if I had an idea of what my future looks like I could more easily let go and keep only the things that would add to the lifestyle I want to have. I could let go easier knowing I was keeping only those things that support my vision. I can't even commit 100 percent to having a garage sale, thinking it has to be perfectly staged. I am so hard on myself."

It was clear to me what was holding Helen back, but she needed to see this before she could take the next step.

I asked Helen what she wanted to bring into her life. Her answer came easily and immediately touched on her emotional clutter: she wanted to release the guilt she carried around not using the abundance of materials she had in her workroom. She felt guilty for "having so much."

Then we focused on what it would feel like if she had her ideal workroom (i.e., a workroom free of clutter). Again, her answer came easily. She would feel more productive, creative and free. Finally, we needed to look at what the overall payoff would be. For Helen, that meant a clearer view of what she wanted her future to be and how to make it happen.

Helen's first steps in clearing her emotional clutter involved identifying what she wanted to feel good about her workroom. It would be an organized space that was visually beautiful, where materials were easy to find and that motivated her to maintain a space where she used things she loved and found homes for what was no longer needed.

Helen and I put a plan into place that helped her identify items other people she knew would love to use for their own projects. This task gave her a great sense of satisfaction that decreased her guilt for not using these wonderful materials. It's when Helen had no idea to whom she could give or donate these items that she became stuck and indecisive.

By removing and "getting rid" of pieces, Helen cleared space in her life for the Universe to bring her what she wanted and needed. Shortly thereafter, she began selling her own work online which raised her self-confidence and self-esteem. No longer was she feeling frustrated or guilty about "how much" she had. By changing the relationship she had with her "stuff," she transformed negative feelings that held her back into positive ones that moved her forward.

TOOL #5

OVERCOMING PERFECTIONISM

"There are only three things you need to let go of: judging, controlling, and being right. Release these three and you will have the whole mind and twinkly heart of a child."

Hugh Prather

As a life coach, I talk with a lot of people who struggle to find happiness. They believe the saying "the grass is always greener on the other side." They don't consider that other people are dealing with the same issues or quest for happiness as they are. As a result of those beliefs, they hold their lives and themselves to impossible standards. In a word, they are perfectionists.

Perfectionism is a type of emotional clutter that holds us tightly in its grip and stops us right in our tracks. We start to do something, but because we continue to redo, rewrite, and redesign over and over, we never finish what we set out to do. Why? because we feel its never good enough. How exhausting is this?

At one time in my life, I was very much a perfectionist. As part my work, I would submit articles to newspapers and magazines (online and off). I also lead and facilitate a large number of workshops and seminars. Even though this is the work I do, I noticed something interesting happening after I'd receive a compliment for something I'd written or at the end of a workshop.

At first, I felt so very appreciative of the kind words; but then came the inner moment of truth where I'd start second-guessing myself and my abilities. The expectations I had for myself and my work were so high, that I always believed that what I'd done could have been done better if I'd put in more effort, added more notes or done more research. I'd begin to wonder whether I measured up to colleagues I admired and if I ever could. (Case in point: I'm having these thoughts even with this book! The voice in the back of my head is not as strong these days, but I do catch it whispering in my ear from time to time.)

When I realized what was happening, it became clear to me that I needed to learn how to let go of perfection and believe that putting forth my best effort—whatever "best" was at the time—was, in fact, valuable.

Now, my motto is "good is good enough," but it wasn't until I truly understood that not only am I not perfect, but that no one is, that I could fully embrace that motto. No longer do I feel the weight of a deadline upon me and begin judging myself. I cheerfully get the work done, revise it if necessary, declare it complete, and move on.

It's not that I stopped caring about the quality of my work. In fact, it's quite the opposite. It's because I care that I'm able to move forward because I've released myself from the chains of perfection.

Exercise: Releasing Perfectionism

Perfectionism likes to wear the disguise of having high standards, but in reality, it's a powerful way in which our inner critic likes to tell us we're not good enough and never will be. To begin the process of quieting that voice and its negative messages, ask yourself the following questions:

1. In what parts of your life do you feel you are a perfectionist?
2. From the list you made above, circle one area and describe what benefit you get from being a perfectionist.
3. What does perfectionism give you that you believe you do not have now?
4. How does being a perfectionist hold you back?

5. If you were to "let go" of being perfect, what fears arise for you?

6. How could you overcome those fears?

7. What would you need to do to begin to let go?

Remember, when we were toddlers, it took practice for us to learn to walk. We just didn't get up and become perfect walkers. We teetered, fell down and got up again. We were not perfect! We stumbled. So unlock those chains of perfection. I guarantee you will be walking with a lighter stride!

TOOL #6

COMMUNICATING CLUTTER

> *"How well we communicate is determined not by how well we say things,*
> *but how well we are understood."*

Andrew Grove

"Steve" and "Mary" were planning to have a conversation one night after work. It was a conversation Mary had asked to have—she wanted to discuss an issue that had been on her mind for some time.

Mary knows that in order for her to have Steve's undivided attention, she has to create an environment free of distractions, so she arranged for their children to spend the next hour at the neighbors' house and asked Steve not to answer the phone during their talk.

Mary's stomach begins to flip as the time approaches, reminding her of the emotional clutter she's carrying into the conversation. Past discussions have never been easy as Steve is technologically tethered to his office. He's become a workaholic and Mary's issue is the negative effect this has had on their relationship and the family.

Mary's anxiety is rooted in a situation we've all experienced—communicating an observation, thought or feeling to someone and what the other person hears is not what we've said... which, in turn, creates more emotional clutter to deal with.

Here are some communication tips* I gave to Mary to foster a productive conversation with Steve:

1. Ensure, to the best of your ability, that there will be no interruptions during your conversation.

 For a list of Sallie's Clutter Tips, go to *www.SoSmartOnline.com/Clutter*

2. Take ownership of your position right away ("This is how I feel...").

3. Do not blame the other person.

4. Be respectful .

5. Take turns talking.

6. Listen.

7. Repeat back what you believe you heard the other person say.

8. Listen again!

9. Don't interrupt when the other person is talking.

10. Be patient.

11. Listen again and again!

12. Be thoughtful.

What I've learned throughout my marriage, is that when my husband and I need to have an important conversation that may be difficult, it's best to begin from a place of feeling. Avoid blaming or accusing—if you don't, the other person is likely to shut down emotionally or worse, go on the attack.

I find it helpful to begin by saying, "This is what I am feeling..." When you start a conversation by saying "This is what you are" or "This is what you do" the conversation turns confrontational almost immediately. The key is to respect each other's voice and hold the space for what the other is feeling.

When I've said my peace, I always ask, "What do you believe you heard me say?" and not "What did you hear me say?" It's a subtle but poignant distinction. The word "believing" allows for some wiggle room—no one needs to parrot back, verbatim, what the other said and the word "hear" connotes a requirement of exactness, one way or another and with no room for interpretation.

The point is that what someone hears you say may not be what you said at all! The listener could only be repeating what he/she wants to hear. So my advice is take the time to listen. If it needs to be repeated, be respectful and thoughtful, for it is not easy to change patterns while communicating.

TOOL #7

FACING YOUR FEAR OF TRYING

"God does not require us to succeed. He only requires that you try."

Mother Teresa

Our vacation was planned; however, it looked like no grass was going to grow under our feet while were visiting our children in Jackson Hole, Wyoming. We had a full and active itinerary and each day we awoke to another day of adventure.

This particular day was one I shall never forget. Our daughter Sarah decided we were going for a hike. Let me say that her description of "hike" was clearly different than mine.

"Mom," she said, "We are going to hike Cody. I want you and Dad to see where we ski. You can see it from the lifts, but I want you to see how steep it is."

I should have known right then and there this was going to be a test…so, should I really go on the hike? Was this an omen?

I watched as our backpacks were being loaded…sandwiches, power bars, fruit, water and more water. I gathered all the clothes, adding layers just in case of bad weather, hopped into the truck Sarah, my husband Conway and I and off we went.

We arrived at Teton Village, headed up the tram to the summit. On the way, discussions had ensued about this so-called "hike." Sarah did her best to reassure me, saying, "Yes, Mom, you can do this, there's only one part that could be challenging, but you'll be fine."

CHALLENGING?! What did THAT mean and why is she only telling me this now? I was beginning to worry about what I was getting into and in that moment, I thought about making my excuses under the guise of not wanting to slow them down. On the other hand, if I turned back, I'd not only be disappointing my daughter, I'd be giving into my fear—my fear of trying (and failing) to complete this hike.

The last thing I wanted to do was set this kind of example for my daughter. The problem was I have a fear of heights and a fear of falling that started when I was 10 years old when my father thought it would be funny to shake the ladder I was climbing to get hay for our horses from the barn. I had no idea how high Sarah was going to take me—would I be teetering on narrow edges of this mountain trail before I plummeted to my death?

The trail itself was compacted with dirt and loose shale. We set about our way and for a while I was doing fine. I had plenty of energy and was eager to keep up with Sarah and Conway. At least until I hit the wall—literally. In front of us was an actual wall of rocks we had to maneuver up a steep grade.

With Sarah and Conway above me, I watched as rocks and shale broke away from the trail and fell below. Was this the time for me to turn around? I seriously considered it. I was being tested physically, but also mentally and emotionally. I put my head down and gritted my teeth; something in me was pulling from an inner strength. I was determined to continue.

Sarah intuitively knew what I was thinking and feeling. I was terrified. I felt my legs tighten and all I could do was repeat to myself, "One step at a time, one step at time, one step…"

My daughter turned to me and said, "Mom, all along these trails I have been able to find fossils. See if you can find one too." She's a smart one, my Sarah. I needed to get my mind off of my fear and focus on something else and fossils were the perfect thing to distract me from my fear.

From that moment forward, my eyes were glued to each shale and broken rock fragment. I not only found many, but began collecting them in my backpack. Although I was still terrified, I allowed myself to feel that fear and invite that feeling to be with me. By embracing it rather than ignoring it, I was able to move through it, including the feelings of nausea, dry mouth and itchiness.

Or so I thought, for not long after this, the trail narrowed even further and the view below was straight down. I'm talking sheer cliffs here. I froze in place and felt the stress response of fear surge through my body. But I was developing a relationship with this fear now, so I was curious how my emotional response was affecting me. And how it was affecting me was a spontaneous breakout of hives on my stomach (so that's why I felt itchy earlier).

I began to slow my breathing, making each breath deep and long and reminding myself that I was safe in this moment, that I had not fallen, and that I was with people who would not take me to a place where I would be harmed. I repeated this like a mantra all the way to the summit. I needed to stay in the present moment and work through this, one step at a time.

Sarah and Conway had crossed over to the "saddle" of Cody, its highest point, to set up for lunch. I lagged behind, staring at the tiny foot-width bit of trail I needed to cross to join them. Neither my daughter nor my husband appeared uneasy or uncomfortable, but in my head I was uttering every expletive I knew!

One deep breath followed another and I told myself, "Sallie, you can do this. You know you can. Look what you've just climbed! Look at what you've already accomplished! You've gone this far, don't give up now. Keep trying, Sallie. You can do this!"

Whether it was my will or my desire not to disappoint my family, I'll never know, but I placed my hands on either side of my face to make blinders so I couldn't see the absence of terra firma on either side of me. Slowly, one step at a time, I moved forward and sooner than I expected, I'd accomplished, what to me, had seemed impossible.

As I sat with my family at the highest point of Cody, I felt victorious. You see, if I had not tried, I wouldn't have stared down my demons or discovered that my emotional turmoil had the power to make my body produce hives. I have always believed what we do fear manifests physically and I was able to see and feel that first hand.

I don't know if this particular success means I've conquered my fear of heights forever, but one thing is for sure, I am certain that no matter what I am faced with, I have the emotional strength to push through to the other side.

If I could pass on one piece of advice, it would be: Don't ever be afraid to try. For you never know what you are actually capable of until you give yourself the chance to prove it to yourself. Even if you don't succeed, you can still walk away with your head held high knowing you at least gave it your best.

Exercise: What Are You Afraid Of?

Write down what type of emotional clutter you are struggling with.

1. What are three things you could do right now to move forward to release its grip?
2. Choose one of those three to act on.
3. When you've taken that action, write down what that felt like.
4. What did you learn about yourself as a result?

TOOL #8

WORKING THROUGH LONELINESS

"We cannot find the light until we acknowledge the darkness. This is called owning."

Mina Parker

It is when you are able to release that which ties or binds your heart, that there becomes room for abundance. As you read through the following letter from my client "Mazzie," do you get the sense of her letting go, embracing the newness of life? Can you see how she felt that "letting go of emotional clutter, frees us up to let go of the physical clutter?"

"Empty nesting is really turning into a fabulous time. It is amazing what you can do when you eliminate the emotional clutter from your mind. May has always been a bittersweet time of year for me—my parents both died in May, my divorce was finalized in the month of May, so there are a lot of significant 'endings' that come up for me when May rolls around.

However, the bright side is that I do feel that this is a time of year that is about rebirth. When someone dies, the days are filled with hope and there is gentleness in the new fresh air that helps restore your life and lets you reflect upon memories sad or happy with the beauty of God's work.

Not too mention the extra work we all put into our gardens after a long winter.

I do think that letting go of emotional clutter, frees us up to let go of the physical clutter. Perhaps that is why so many of us dream of white condos with white furniture everywhere? Sounds like heaven. No muss no fuss."

Exercise: Shifting Out of Loneliness

Write down where you have loneliness in your life?

1. What does it bring you?
2. Why do you need it?
3. What would get in your way of moving away from loneliness?
4. How can you prevent this from happening?
5. If you were not lonely, what would you like to see your life to be?
6. What is something positive you could do to be less lonely?
7. When will you begin?

TOOL #9

RELEASING GUILT

"When considering change, remember — there is an emotional connection necessary for people to commit to new ways."

Stacy Aaron

My client "Lorna" wanted to move to California, but felt the emotional clutter of the ties to family and friends who wanted her to stay in the East. She worked long and hard researching her options, making hard choices (and feeling guilty all the while) only to see her goals, passion and vision come to fruition.

Lorna was in her late 20s and very much connected to her family. She loved their traditions and her large family; though she was clearly not happy with her job. She called me and asked if I would work with her. I asked her straight away, "What was it she wanted?" Lorna explained that her heart has gravitated to the Napa Valley region for as long as she can remember. To her it was a "spiritual" place. It brought her peace and provided her with the most beautiful landscape with which to continue her professional photography.

Problem: How was she going to break away from her family of origin without feeling guilty or letting them down? Her family continually discouraged her to leave as she had no job in California, no transportation, no housing and knew no one. All of this made Lorna anxious and she began to have second thoughts of her dream ever coming to fruition.

Solution: So having gained her trust, I slowly began to ask Lorna to step out of her comfort zone. At first she hesitated…it was more comfortable to not make a decision than make one. Over and over her hearts desire kept floating to the surface. I asked her if she could really listen to what it was saying and journal about it. She did and did it well.

She discovered a variety of things within herself: 1) she needed to find HER voice when confronting her family about her dream; 2) she applied specific techniques setting boundaries within conversations; 3) we created a plan for her week by week; and 4) she began to investigate and research the Napa Valley and its offerings.

We came up with: a budget plan: how much she needed to save and how much she needed live on. She needed to find a temporary living space (bed and breakfasts), explore part time jobs, rental cars vs. public transportation and take the "pulse" of her heart.

Was she as in love with the region as before? Did this Mecca continue to call to her? Lorna was meticulous working with what she researched, discounting and crossing off all areas that would not work for her. At one point, I challenged her to fly out and drive around. Get a better feeling and more clarity. To be right there, present in the land.

She did! And upon her return she called to say she had made up her mind; she was to move at the first of the year. She broke the news to her parents, relatives and friends. I believe that was the most difficult part of this process.

What she learned most of all was to listen to her inner voice, not the clutter of her mental mind running the tape, "How am I possibly going to move, what do I need to do, this is overwhelming." But she listened to her emotional side, telling her far within her to follow her dreams. She watched and felt her body respond when arriving in Napa, the smile which came over her face. As she said to me, "I'm home."

Here's what Lorna had to say some months after moving her life across the country:

"I had this dream, for several years, to live in Napa Valley and finally after years of thinking about it, I did it. I was afraid to take that leap out of the comfortable state in my life and into what I loved and dreamed of over and over again. Why did it take me so long? I'll never know.

Now a year and half later, after having moved here to Napa Valley, I am unbelievably excited and loving every minute of it. I have a very successful career in the world of social media for a winery, have continued to build my photography client base with very prestigious wineries, and have so many new friends throughout the valley.

If I were to offer any advice to someone reading this, I would say go with what is in your heart. Sallie, you always reminded me to think of it as 'what speaks to your heart':

1. *How does this affect your body's response?*

2. *Listen to your body.*

3. *Listen to your heart.*

4. *And go with your intuition.*

When I have ups and downs, I often think of my accomplishments and where I came from. I remember to believe in myself and stay in line with my goals and dreams. The more you believe in yourself, the more you find the positive, the more the world opens up for you with very little effort. You can do anything you put your mind to. Thank you so much, Sallie."

Exercise: Lessening Guilt

1. Write down what type of guilt clutter you are struggling with.

2. What are three things you could do right now to move forward to relieve the guilt?

3. Choose one of those three to take action on.

4. Write down what it felt like to take that action.

5. What did you learn about yourself?

TOOL #10
LET THE FUTURE BE THE FUTURE

> *"I never think of the future—it comes soon enough."*

Albert Einstein

"Jane" is married, mother to a young son and works full time. Our coaching sessions focused on the relationship between her emotional and physical clutter—she had a hard time letting go of things she collected because she worried that without them, her son would not know who she was or what mattered to her. Here's part of Jane's story, in her own words:

> *"Yes, I have great difficulty in letting go of some of the things I have collected. I have spent quite some time thinking about my habits and usually have to laugh and roll my eyes gently at myself. I forgive myself for my cluttery actions, but would like to change some underlying behavior... I think there are some emotional reasons why I collect what I do, which I will try to explain in a second.*

> *About a year ago, I gleaned greater understanding into why I was doing what I was doing when I asked for advice. I was about to ask someone for suggestions, when it dawned on me that I really wanted to save the newspaper articles and clippings for my son in a scrapbook, so that at some point – perhaps after I was gone, or perhaps before – he could look through them and find out 'what kind of person I was.' What mattered to me? What did I feel passionate about?"*

Jane said she realized that she was "afraid" her son might not know who she was, in case she died the next day that he might remember bits and pieces of her but he wouldn't "know" her. Another realization Jane had was that her own mother had not saved anything for her when she was growing up. Jane felt she was missing parts of her mother by not having long-ago objects her "hopelessly sentimental" self could hold onto.

Jane goes onto say:

> *"I have been getting better about finding new homes for items...I am taking some of my son's old clothes and toys to a consignment shop and using the money from those sales to buy him what he needs now. Schools are also wonderful takers of things, and I will ask them if I may bring frames for children's' artwork, etc. Still, there is so much more, and I am not quite sure how to tackle it all. Old animal welfare magazines might actually go to the library of a newly formed "Animal Law" department at the University! THOSE are the connections I would love to make... where things that still have value might get used by those who value them.*
>
> *I know that with patience and with regularly setting aside enough time per week, I will start to whittle away at the piles. Will I ever NOT be able to read a newspaper without a handy pair of scissors? I don't know about that!"*

Learning this about Jane (and from Jane), my response needed to acknowledge that she was coming directly from her heart—the place where I sense she lived.

The value Jane placed on having things be valued and be OF value was very strong and the desire she had for her son to be able to really know her if something happened to her was very real.

In order to release this fear of not being known, I told Jane about a folder I keep in my own home simply labeled "Personal." In it, I've put articles, sayings, excerpts from my own journals, and other writings that my adult children will read one day before or after I'm gone.

I also reminded her gently that her son is learning who she is NOW. He sees what is important to her by the examples she sets every day. Children are very intuitive and in touch with who we are; you see this when suddenly the words you say without thinking start coming out of their mouths.

Finally, I congratulated her on the steps she'd taken to part with various items she'd collected. "Worry not, Jane," I said, "his memories of you will be with him and through the stories of others forever."

TOOL #11

MOVING PAST FRUSTRATION

'I've come to believe that all my past failure and frustrations were actually laying the foundation for the understandings that have created the new level of living I now enjoy."

Tony Robbins

I'm often asked whether emotional or mental clutter is what makes it difficult to maintain the necessary focus to clear the debris from our minds or our environment, thus bringing about feelings of frustration.

I believe the answer to this, to some degree, is both. The clutter in our hearts and our heads can be a great source of frustration when we can't move through it and that frustration can lead to anxiety (*how will I ever get this done?*) and to feeling overwhelmed (*there's so much to do, I don't know where to begin*).

De-cluttering is challenging enough, but even more challenging for individuals who already deal with Attention Deficit Disorder (ADD) and are acutely aware of the distractions lurking around every corner.

"Carol" was feeling over-tired, overworked and overwhelmed with the clutter. On top of that she was caring for two elderly dogs. Here is her story:

'I'm busy and frustrated at work, arrive home between 6 and 7pm (sometimes later if I have errands to run) and need to care for my two elderly dogs. I do the necessary things, but the junk mail I need to sort, file and/or shred piles up. I don't have 'homes' for some things and I don't want to spend the only free time I have on weekends cleaning my house.

I'm taking a week off soon and hope to hire someone to help me organize and deep clean the house as well as put some new storage solutions into place. Maybe I'll hire a coach to help keep me accountable and teach me how to move through this systematically.

In the meantime, I'm researching job options that allow me to work less and have more time. Getting organized would definitely help—it's just DOING it that's the problem."

Problem: "Carol" is busy and frustrated at work, gets home later than she'd like and has little time to herself.

Solution: She states she could hire a coach, get someone in to help organize and clean, possibly look for a new job so she could have more time for "ME" but her conflict remains—how to motivate herself to make all of this happen.

TOOL #12

HOW TO CLEAR YOUR CLUTTER

"Just as your car runs more smoothly and requires less energy to go faster and farther when the wheels are in perfect alignment, you perform better when your thoughts, feelings, emotions, goals, and values are in balance."

Brian Tracy

Exercise: Fill IN the Blanks

To get a clearer picture of what emotional clutter you might be storing in your heart, read the following sentences:

1. I am tolerating or continue to tolerate...

2. Things I do that are not supporting and serving me are...

3. The habits I've created and am stuck with out of fear are...

Exercise: Open Your Heart

You may recognize parts of this exercise from Chapter 2, when I walked you through how to clear your mental clutter, but when it comes to changing old patterns into new, healthier habits, repetition and consistency are your best weapons.

WHERE DO YOU START? Right where you stand, right now, not tomorrow, but here in the present moment. Take a deep breath in through your nose; blow out from your mouth. Do this three times (it will began to relax you).

Step 1 Set Yourself Up for Success

Limit your clearing sessions to anywhere from 15 minutes up to three hours, but no more. Why am I asking you to put a limit on it? I want you to be successful here. I don't want failure—I want success. A useful way to stick to this is to play your favorite music in the background. Usually, it takes 45 minutes to an hour for a CD to finish and you can commit to clearing until the CD is over.

Step 2 Limit Distractions

Next, it is absolutely necessary to limit distractions. So, if you need to go to the bathroom, or you're hungry or thirsty, take care of it before you start. I also don't want you to look at your computer, answer your cell phone, your landline, the doorbell, check e-mail or anything else. And don't even try texting! When you're clearing, I want you to clear with no distractions at all.

When we release clutter in our minds, our emotional clutter tends to follow suit. We feel less stressed, less burdened and more at peace. This exercise is just the beginning, but done regularly, it has lasting results.

Step 3 Get Ready to Write

Make sure when you start your clearing process you have the right tools in place. When you're dealing with emotional cutter, a notepad and a pen to write (or your computer with email and browser closed, please) is the way to go. The goal is to keep the clutter flowing freely out of you and onto the paper. Get it out—all of it.

By writing down what is in our heart, whether it be wanting to forgive, wanting to release resentment, worry or whatever it is for you, you become less stressed, less burdened and more at peace. Why? Because it (the thoughts and its energy) is physically out of your body, you have released those thoughts onto the paper. I am not saying that they have disappeared forever, but this is the START.

Step 4 Naming Your Desires

Now that you've emptied your heart onto the page, spend a few minutes thinking and writing about what you want to bring into your life. What do you want emotionally? A better relationship with someone? More peace, happiness or kindness? What about more compassion or acceptance? What is it exactly for you? Pick up that pen or computer and—you guessed it—write it down.

Step 5 Creating Space for What You Want

Using a fresh sheet of paper, now list all the things you want to REMOVE from your life. Be as specific and complete as you can. Do you want to let go of hurts, grudges or resentment? What about unresolved conflicts or difficult relationships? Do you need to let go of fear, your perfectionism or negative self talk?

Refer to this list several times this week and reflect on why it's important for you to remove these particular pieces of clutter. Remember, when you rid your life of something that no longer serves you, whether it's a thought pattern, behavior or object, you create space for more of what you DO want to come into your life. If you hold onto everything, there's no room for that positive energy to enter.

Chapter Five
Motivation Tools: Feeling The Effects of Clutter

*"Our ultimate freedom is the right and power to decide
how anybody or anything outside ourselves will affect us."*

Stephen R. Covey

Throughout the previous chapters, I've delved into the specifics of what mental, physical and emotional clutter is by using my own stories and those of my clients as poignant examples. If you were reading between the lines, then you also started to pick up on the price these three forms of clutter ask us to pay—the real cost of having clutter in our lives.

TOOL #1
MENTAL CLUTTER COST CALCULATOR

"The simplification of one's life is one of the steps to inner peace. A persistent simplification will create an inner and outer well being that places harmony in one's life."

Peace Pilgrim

In Chapter 1, I posed the question: "If you are feeling disorganized and/or unproductive, which form of clutter do you start with first?" The three forms of clutter are interrelated and most often, trying to identify the origin of your clutter follows "the-chicken-or-the-egg" logic. Which form came first? Is that where we start? Trying to answer those questions is just another form of mental clutter. It doesn't matter where you start; it only matters that you start.

Let's review the signs of mental clutter:

- My mind never shuts off.
- My mental to-do list is a mile long.
- I can't let go of thinking, even when I put my head on the pillow at night.
- I often forget appointments, what I need at the grocery store or why I walked into the other room.
- I feel like I a have to do "everything."
- I frequently tolerate situations that are stressful.
- I feel unable to keep up.

- I feel pressured to be superhuman.
- I find myself procrastinating.
- I rarely say "no" to requests.
- I am always overdoing, over-scheduling and over-committing
- I find myself doing things I don't want to out of fear or guilt.

If this sounds like you, take heart. Recognizing that you've got a problem with mental clutter is the first step in beginning to rid yourself of this excess baggage before it begins to seep into the rest of your life. And remember, mental clutter is most often the result of overdoing, over-scheduling and over-committing. It's also that tape that loops through our head playing the song "Shoulda, Woulda, Coulda."

What do you think this does to your body, mind and spirit? I'll tell you what it does:

It lays the foundation for you to become an over-stressed, over-scheduled, over-exhausted and over-stimulated person who is vulnerable to DIS-EASE.

If we don't clear our mental clutter, it breeds, taking up more and more of our precious energy and resources than is healthy. If we don't find a way to clear this clutter on a regular basis, we risk storing it in our bodies and allowing it to deplete us further.

"Phyllis" had written a book and found herself needing to market and promote it, but hesitated, even though she knew what she needed to do and the timeframe in which everything needed to happen. After talking with her for an hour, she wrote:

"I want to thank you from the bottom of my heart for that wonderful hour I spent with you this summer. Thank you for giving me the chance to practice two things that don't come easily to me: asking for help and asking the help of people who already have a lot to do in their own lives."

So what might have happened if Phyllis had chosen NOT to ask for help and allowed the mental clutter around her book to stay as is?

1. She would be disappointed by lack of sales.
2. All the efforts of writing this book would have been in vain.
3. She probably would have abandoned her plans to write another book.
4. She would have remained scared to go out of her comfort zone and ask for help.
5. She would continue to feel she was a burden to others.
6. Her stress levels would have increased.

Phyllis and I discussed what would happen if she actually asked for help from the people who could help her—what would she learn about herself and how would that effect her mental clutter? She said:

"Oh my goodness—what a wonderful question, Sallie. Right off the bat, I discovered what fabulous resources already exist in my life in and through so many of the people that I know. I was also reminded how empowering and helpful it is to simply ask about what others might know that I do not."

Did you notice the change not only in her tone of her quote but in the THOUGHTS that she expressed?

Exercise: Putting a Price on Your Mental Clutter

Take out your journal and choose a situation that's part of your mental clutter, then answer the following questions below.

1. What is your mental clutter "costing" you?
2. How is it affecting you?
3. What could you do differently to be more proactive and remove the effects?

TOOL #2

PHYSICAL CLUTTER COST CALCULATOR

"The concept of total wellness recognizes that our every thought, word, and behavior affects our greater health and well-being. And we, in turn, are affected not only emotionally but also physically and spiritually."

Greg Anderson

By now you know that clutter works from the inside out, but how is your physical clutter affecting you? Besides consuming literal space, physical clutter has far-reaching mental, emotional and physiological effects.

Physical clutter robs us of the ability to think in a free-flowing way. The more clutter there is around us, the longer and louder that to-do list running through our heads becomes. How do you expect to find balance and peace if you're constantly looking for items you can't find? More likely, you're experiencing increased feelings of frustration, irritation and being overwhelmed and all those feelings do create more stress.

That stress now resides in your body producing toxins. Remember "Marsha" from Chapter 3? She was a hoarder and the physical environment that resulted from extreme physical clutter actually caused her to become ill. Even if you are not a hoarder, your physical clutter around you binds and holds you within the confines of not only yourself but your space. There is no room to grow, to spread your wings, to be the best you can be.

Let's revisit parts of "Marsha's" story this time with an eye on how her clutter affected her health and led to life-threatening behaviors:

> *"My life was so out of control, in every aspect, that I was getting critically ill from it. I was so overwhelmed that it affected my whole being...every single day. All kinds of things suffered as result...my relationships, my personality, my interaction with people, my friendships, my performance at work to name a few....*
>
> *....My health and breathing problems physically prevented me from being able to work through it! It was so bad that I almost died at home at least twice due to lack of oxygen in my lungs and heart...because I refused to have anyone come into my home—friend, neighbor, EMT, or a stranger. I refused to let them see the entrance to my apartment, never mind all that it held.....*
>
> *....I refused to go to the hospital for fear they would KEEP me and someone would see my apartment because they would have to take care of my pets.*
>
> *The embarrassment and horribleness of it all weighed me down to the point it was intolerable: living in such chaos and turmoil was physically and psychologically exhausting, beyond belief.*
>
> *In addition I suffered severe financial problems due to not keeping jobs due to poor concentration (I wonder why) and being worn out (feeling like my home was a second and third, and fourth job) Just wading through things and trying to find things daily in order to function (function at a minimal existence, by the way) ."*

What price did Marsha pay for her physical clutter?

1. Her physical space was out of control and inhabitable:
2. Her life felt out of control and she was a prisoner in her own apartment.
3. Her surroundings were making her critically ill.
4. Her health was at risk.
5. Her breathing problems escalated.
6. Her nutritional habits were obsolete
7. Her relationships, her personality, her friendships and performance at work suffered leading to her losing her job.

8. Losing her job added another dimension to the stress of her finances.

9. Emotionally she was physically exhausted.

10. She felt ashamed.

11. She was mentally frustrated.

12. She became depressed.

13. She lacked the focus or motivation to do anything.

Then there was "Sam" who was not the neatest creature of habit. His side of the bedroom looked as if it could have been a locker room…socks, gym shorts and jersey on the floor. The latest newspaper and sports magazines found a home on the scatter rug below his side of the bed. Then there was the exercise equipment. How could he or his wife truly relax and rest with all of this clutter around?

In this scenario, physical and mental clutter have gotten together and invited emotional clutter to their little party. Everywhere Sam and his wife look in their bedroom, they're overwhelmed. The situation causes anxiety that makes true rest impossible.

Here's how "Sam" and his wife defined the cost of their physical clutter:

1. There's "no room to breathe."

2. There's "no room to rest."

3. Everywhere we look, we see chaos.

4. We feel chaotic in the room.

5. Our bodies and minds are anxious, unable to relax.

Remember the time we spent talking about the important role of kitchens and dining rooms in our lives? What do you think the cost of not dealing with clutter in those areas is?

1. These rooms become pit stops and "drive-thru" areas rather than places we gather in order to connect and relax.

2. As a result of having no calm place in which to gather, we become unsettled.

3. We eat more on the run, in front of the television or the computer; these quick hits affect the quality of our nutrition and intake of GOOD foods.

4. Our poor food choices don't fuel our bodies properly, so we lack the energy to get through the day.

5. We become disconnected from family and friends, losing quality time spent in conversation and sharing.

We also talked about how physical clutter in my home office affects me. If I walk away from a messy desk, I know when I return to work at it in the morning I'm going to feel scattered and have trouble focusing. Physical clutter affects me by limiting my ability to be productive. Additionally, if I don't take a few minutes at the end of the day to plan for tomorrow, I have difficulty quieting my mind, which makes for a restless night.

Case in point: While I've been writing this book, stacks of paper have been multiplying around me. The solution was clear to me that I had to find a way to tame these piles of paper until the book was done. How did I do this? I implemented a strategy I call "out of sight, out of mind - but only for the time being."

I took a twin-sized white sheet from my linen closet and draped it over all the papers, books, magazines I used for my research so when I entered my home office, I saw a "cleaner" area. This allowed me not to get distracted by the mess and get my writing done. When I finish the book, I'll set about re-organizing and filing all of these materials using the SMART goals system, because here's what happens if I don't:

1. The sight of all the stacks of paper will make my head spin.
2. I will feel discomfort in the pit in my stomach.
3. The longer the piles sit, the more they'll grate on my nerves and I'll become irritated and cranky.
4. I'll feel totally at loose ends, unorganized.
5. I'll feel unprepared for the day and every day the piles remain, which means I'll be unfocused and unproductive.
6. I won't feel energized or fresh.
7. I'll feel that I'm not giving my best to my clients or other projects, a message my inner critic loves to deliver.

Exercise: Putting a Price on Your Physical Clutter

Take out your journal and choose a situation that's part of your physical clutter, then answer the following questions below:

1. What is your physical clutter "costing" you?
2. How is it affecting you?
3. What could you do differently to be more proactive and remove the effects?

TOOL #3

EMOTIONAL CLUTTER COST CALCULATOR

"Take control of your consistent emotions and begin to consciously and deliberately reshape your daily experience of life."

Anthony Robbins

Emotional clutter comes straight from the heart. It includes the feelings surrounding past and present issues we haven't yet processed, worked through, nurtured or released. Emotional clutter is:

- The need to be perfect
- The need to be right
- Self-defeating behaviors
- Overinflated expectations

As I said before, I believe emotional clutter lives in the very center of the heart, affecting our sense of self and our self-esteem. This clutter comes from a deep place within you and plays a powerful role in both your health and well-being because, like all clutter, emotional clutter weighs us down, makes us feel trapped, overwhelms and exhausts us.

We might experience emotional clutter in the form of feeling over-stressed and overburdened, betrayed, scared, insecure, angry—the list goes on. If you can feel it, it can become emotional clutter.

Emotional clutter robs us of:

- Our sense of self
- Our energy
- Our joy
- Our productivity
- Our effectiveness
- Our true authenticity
- Our happiness
- Our sense of peace
- Our efficiency
- Our balance

Remember "Betty" from Chapter 4? "Betty" had spent the last couple of years trying to rebuild a relationship with her sisters after a big blowout. She wanted to reach out, but was scared because she believed her sisters would probably not accept her invitation to spend the Christmas holidays with her family. In order to clear this clutter, "Betty" took the risk and offered the invitation. If you recall, here's what happened:

> *"This year's holidays will be simplified, to a certain, sad extent, since both of my sisters have opted not to come down to celebrate. I was saddened by the news, but was not surprised; since last year's tyrannical explosive outbursts on their part left me deeply shaken. (It has taken almost a year to forgive them!) I called them on Thanksgiving and at least we had civil conversations. Well, it does simplify matters!"*

Even though Betty's sisters turned down her invitation—as she suspected they would—she still felt sad. But that sadness was really the release of the emotional clutter that had built up from not reaching out to them. With this hurdle behind her, Betty could now prepare for the holidays focused on her family and how they would celebrate the season. Additionally, Betty learned that she and her sisters could now hold civil conversations together, rather than stew in silence.

If she hadn't cleared this emotional clutter, Betty may have continued to feel:

1. Sadness
2. Guilt
3. Unwanted
4. Unheard
5. Lonely

Exercise: Putting a Price on Your Emotional Clutter

Take out your journal and choose a situation that's part of your emotional clutter, then answer the following questions below:

1. What is your physical clutter "costing" you?
2. How is it affecting you?
3. What could you do differently to be more proactive and remove the effects?

> *"As human beings we all want to be happy and free from misery… we have learned that the key to happiness is inner peace. The greatest obstacles to inner peace are disturbing emotions such as anger, attachment, fear and suspicion, while love and compassion and a sense of universal responsibility are the sources of peace and happiness."*

The Dalai Lama

Chapter Six
Belief Tools: What Do You Believe?

"It's not what they did.
It's what you believe about what they did that hurts."

Brooke Castillo

TOOL #1

IDENTIFYING YOUR "MIS-BELIEVES"

"It's not who you are that holds you back;
it's who you think you're not."

Author Unknown

We are all born unique, healthy and whole. No two of us are the same. We all have specific talents and gifts to offer. We can choose to release the bonds of old beliefs and rejoice or we can allow our "mis-believes" to steer us into our future. The choice is ours, alone, but we have to confront our own demons and inner critics to get back our authentic selves.

I want to show you how past experiences and memories can hold us back and how we can take in false perceptions of who we are if—and only if—we continue to allow these "mis-believes" to take our power.

Here are just a few of those untrue "negative beliefs" that I have heard from my clients. As you read through the list, pay special attention to the ones that ring true in your heart. Put a star next to them or jot them down on a piece of paper or in your journal.

I am worthless.	I am dumb.
I am unattractive.	I am a failure.
I am ugly.	I am not a priority.
I am friendless.	No one cares for me.
I am not normal.	I am a burden.
I am different.	I am weak.
I am not smart enough.	I will always be alone.
I am stupid.	I will forever struggle.
I am defective.	I will always be fat.
I am mentally slow.	I am unlikable.

TOOL #2

RECLAIMING YOUR POWER

"If you really put a small value on yourself, rest assured that the
world will not raise your price."

Author Unknown

Review the list of untrue thoughts that rang true for you. These represent
your overall beliefs about yourself. Now let's take the "S" from what we
learned from our SMART goals and get specific about how these beliefs
make you feel and affect your self-esteem and behaviors. The "S" here also
stands for self discovery—your goal is to get specific about why you feel
these beliefs are true.

Get out your journal and work through the following series of questions that
most apply to you. Take your time and be ruthlessly honest—no one will see
this except for you.

1. I am worthless.
    a. Where in your body do you feel worthless?
    b. Why do you believe you feel worthless?
    c. What is the truth?
2. I am unattractive.
    a. Where do you believe you feel unattractive?
    b. Where do you believe those words originate?
    c. What is the truth?
3. I am ugly.
    a. Where do you believe it to have originated?
    b. How do you believe you feel ugly?
    c. What is the truth?
4. I am friendless.
    a. What makes you believe that?
    b. Why do you believe this is true?
    c. What is the lie?

5. I am not normal.

   a. Why do you believe that?

   b. Where did those words originate?

   c. What is the real truth?

6. I am different.

   a. What makes you believe that?

   b. Why do you believe this is true?

   c. What is the lie?

7. I am not smart enough.

   a. What makes you believe that?

   b. Why do you believe this is true?

   c. What is the lie?

8. I am stupid.

   a. Where did you hear those words?

   b. What weight does it carry for you?

   c. What is your real truth?

9. I am defective.

   a. What parts of yourself do you feel are defective?

   b. When did you believe this?

   c. What is the real truth?

10. I am mentally slow.

    a. Where did you hear those words?

    b. What makes you believe it so?

    c. What is the real truth?

11. I am dumb.

    a. Where do you believe this to be true?

    b. How have the words affected you?

    c. What is your real truth?

12. I am a failure.

    a. When do you believe you last failed?

    b. How has this supported you?

    c. What is the real truth?

13. I am not a priority.

    a. Why do you believe you are NOT a priority?

    b. What part of your inner critic is speaking?

    c. What is the real truth?

14. No one cares for me.

    a. Where did this feeling arise from?

    b. How do you believe that to be so?

    c. What is your real truth?

15. I am a burden.

    a. Where do you believe that to be so?

    b. How is that affecting your life?

    c. What is your real truth?

16. I am weak.

    a. Where do you believe this to be so?

    b. What part of you feels weak?

    c. What is the real truth?

17. I will always be alone.

    a. When did this belief arise?

    b. How is this supporting your belief?

    c. What is the real truth?

18. I will forever struggle.

    a. How has this belief served you?

    b. What is your true struggle?

    c. What is the real truth?

19. I will always be fat.

    a. Where did those words originate?

    b. What weight do they hold for you?

    c. What is the real truth?

20. I am unlikable.

    a. What parts of yourself do you like?

    b. What aspects of yourself do you believe others would like?

    c. What is the real truth?

TOOL #3
CHANGING YOUR THOUGHTS

> *"What a man thinks of himself, that it is which determines,*
> *or rather indicates his fate."*

Henry David Thoreau

Now that you've identified what your negative thought patterns are and spent some time unraveling where they come from and how they make you feel, let's turn them around into **positive affirmations**.

1. I am worthy to care for myself and others.

2. I am attractive and glowing.

3. I am beautiful inside and out.

4. I have many friends who love me.

5. I am as normal as any other human being.

6. I am special with unique gifts.

7. I go comfortably at my own pace.

8. I am smart and applaud my learning style.

9. I am never broken, I just get stronger.

10. I like going at my own speed.

11. I am intelligent and use it wisely.

12. I learn from my mistakes.

13. I am my own priority; I cherish who I am.

14. I am amazed how supportive family and friends are to me.

15. I am someone who people want to help.

16. I am strong.

17. I will never be alone, I am loved.

18. I will forever have learning moments and succeed.

19. I will nurture myself today and always.

20. I have much to offer in friendship.

Exercise: Positive Affirmations

Self-doubt is a natural part of being human. While our negative, self-critical thoughts may never go away entirely, we always have the power to change them. So the next time you catch yourself having a negative thought, I challenge you to:

1. Write down what that negative thought is.

2. Identify where it's coming from and/or from whose voice it originates.

3. Turn that negative thought into a positive affirmation—write it down!

Repeat the affirmation often and/or put it on sticky notes to post on mirrors, doors or in the car—anywhere you'll see it repeatedly until it takes root.

TOOL #4

EXCAVATING YOUR PAST

"No one can make you feel inferior without your permission."

Eleanor Roosevelt

In a lot of ways, I feel that I have lived a "privileged" life. By that, I don't mean I was born with a silver spoon in my mouth or that every one of my wishes magically came true. It's more the feeling I get from the memories of my childhood: days soaked in the smell of the outdoors, riding my horse for hours on end through the fields and woods, sitting on my father's lap cutting hay in the early evenings and playing in the barn. But I also mean knowing that I had the love and support of both of my parents as well as the company of my four sisters.

That doesn't mean I didn't have my own struggles. I certainly did! And those struggles helped me to mold the beliefs I had about myself which honestly, weren't very loving.

In my mind, I was:

Not pretty enough

Not hip enough

Not smart enough

Notice the repetition of the word "enough." It wasn't that I didn't possess these qualities, but that I was measuring myself against some other ideal rather than celebrating my strengths.

I'm going to take you through my own journey with my "mis-believes" and show you how this mental and emotional clutter contributed to what I believed about myself.

Why am I sharing these very personal stories? In order for us to get past the hurt we have to walk through it. We can be hurt physically, emotionally and mentally; as children we believe only what we see is true.

As children, if our parents criticize us, we believe we are not worthy. If our teachers say, "You don't measure up," we think we are less than smart. If friends say, "You are too fat, too skinny, too tall, too short, full of pimples" or physically "unattractive" than we believe WE ARE. We take it at face value.

It is not that these struggles have made me who I am now, it is the learning in the event and who I become out of the struggles that bring me the most meaning!

This is important in choosing to understand your beliefs about yourself.

Not Pretty Enough (Sallie's "Physical" Clutter)

Among my sisters, my birth order within the five of us is number four. My oldest sister, Nina, is 10 years older than I am and I have only vague memories of the time when all of us lived at home. I do remember though she had her OWN room of which I was forever jealous. Mostly, I remember her in the barn—like me, she loved to ride—or visiting home on her breaks from boarding school.

My second oldest sister Taffy—I have more clear memories of her. Taffy was the "cute" one, petite figure skater with a striking pug nose and perfectly coifed hair. Every night before bed, she did her "do" with bristled curlers that made it look like she was laying a head of armor down on the pillow only to wake up looking gorgeous in the morning.

I envied Taffy's looks. She was stunning to me. And yet, it was with her that I had my very first fistfight, an all-out slugfest. I'm not sure how old I was, but I know I was young and that I was feeling so angry at her because I wanted to be JUST LIKE HER.

My physical appearance, I felt, was hampered by bunions, for which I was teased. I remember my feet always looking "normal" to me, but the reality was every night I had to wear "bunion straighteners" that my parents bought out of a catalog ...oh how pretty! I also had buck teeth, so add in the braces and I was quite a sight.

On top of that, all the work I did to take care of the horses—carrying water buckets, shoveling hay, mucking stalls—gave me highly developed bicep muscles. To make matters worse, I also inherited a set of overactive sweat glands that made wearing short sleeve shirts, a dress or even a bathing suit emotionally uncomfortable (more teasing, especially from classmates).

To say I was self conscious was an understatement.

I remember distinctly, one Sunday afternoon when the family gathered together for lunch. My grandmother said, "Taffy is the prettiest, Gretchen is the loneliest and Sallie is the homeliest."

I was speechless, embarrassed, mortified and waited for someone to come to my defense. No one did, no one said a word; they all laughed, all except me! I was no more than 12 or 13 years old - an impressionable age - and that comment has stayed with me my entire life.

Exercise: Find Your Inner Beauty

1. Write down what in your past has made you believe you are LESS than beautiful.
2. Define your definition of beautiful, inner and outer.
3. Now write down your new definition of beauty.

It took me years to come to terms with "I am who I am." I may still have my bunions, my buckteeth have been straightened, my biceps may not be as pronounced, but I know if I put my mind to it, I have the ability to be successful.

I want to make something very clear here....those physical aspects are not who we are! Those are not our values. It's our values that determine the kind of person we are. No one can take that away from us...no one; unless you allow it!

Not Hip Enough (Sallie's "Emotional" Clutter)

Growing up in the 1960s and early 1970s, I was considered by my teenage friends to be the "square" one. I had no desire to do dope or drink; it never interested me "to get high" or "blackout." I watched them, continued to be part of the group, but clearly felt different and when I heard them say things like, "What's wrong with you?" and "You're no fun;" I felt judged.

At that point I retreated, found a smaller group of friends and became shyer. When you are in your mid-teens these words hurt more deeply than anyone knows.

Who was I? What was I supposed to be if I didn't want to be just like them doing what they were doing? That was the inner struggle. What did I want? Where was my voice?

Well, I had learned at a very early age that my voice was not heard. I was nicknamed "the emotional one" in the family.

"Sallie's being emotional."

"Sallie's overreacting."

"Sallie, it's not as bad as all that..."

At times it was easier to keep to myself. I found our animals were my best ears; they knew my darkest secrets, my joys and my heartaches.

Here's what I learned over the years: it's precisely because I am the "emotional one" that I have the ability to listen intently to my clients while having compassion for their struggles. My success here is, in part, because I choose to recognize being emotional as a positive trait, not a negative one. The word "emotional" has no negative connotation for me any longer. It's because I choose to believe that being emotional isn't a bad quality.

"Miss Emotion" has served me well—we go way back, paddling the canoe together. Whether we hit rough waters, fast currents or lose our compass course, we will not relinquish our paddles. Yes, we might take on water or fall out of the canoe but we will not give up our power.

Exercise: Finding Your Gifts

1. Make a list of all the negative beliefs which you BELIEVE you have.

2. Make a list of all the positive characteristics and values that YOU POSSESS.

3. Look at the difference between the two and protect your gifts, for these beliefs are true.

Not Smart Enough (Sallie's "Mental" Clutter)

Back in the "dark ages" or "prehistoric times" as my kids jokingly used to call it, school was not easy for me. I excelled in art, but reading and math were challenging. I wished I knew then what I know now, but then again I would not have experienced the learning or growth of self.

All through my elementary education (Grades 1-5) my report cards always read, "Sallie continues to put in 100 percent effort, however, her reading comprehension is not comparable to her classmates. She fails to identify key elements in the stories or lessons, underlining much and becoming frustrated when trying to recite what she read."

But I excelled in ART! (No one wanted to talk about that.)

My parents hired a tutor for me and I had to cut back on the time I spent with my horse. I was not happy by a long shot. If I felt different from my classmates already, this just made me feel more different. Doing my homework and studying took longer for me than anyone else (or so it seemed). I truly believed I was dumb.

But I knew I excelled in ART! (Still, no one wanted to talk about that.)

I remember just as if it were yesterday, when I was summoned to my parents' bedroom. It was just a week before the first day of school when I would be entering the sixth grade. My mother was holding a letter in her hands and she read it aloud to me. It was from the school and it said:

"We feel it is in Sallie's best interest to repeat the fifth grade. Another year of reading comprehension will serve her well."

This cemented it for me: I was dumb!

The first day of school came. All the students gathered in the auditorium of our small school where the principal read off students' names and assigned grades and teachers to each one. He started with the first graders and continued on up. When he read the names for fifth grade and mine was among them, the heads of my former classmates moving up to sixth grade turned to stare.

I hadn't shared this news with anyone. My classmates looked shocked and I felt humiliated and embarrassed. I might as well have tattooed the word "DUMB" on my forehead for the whole world to see. That was what I was feeling.

But I knew I excelled in ART! (And still, no one wanted to talk about it.)

The next few years weren't easy for me, especially when it came to math. Math and I were like oil and vinegar. I could never wrap my head around the equations. What do you mean there is only ONE right way to do a problem? I often came up with many solutions, but not the "right" ones for my teacher, Mr. Motram.

His solution was to have me correct my errors that were present in my homework or my tests on Saturday mornings—10 times each! If I got them wrong again, I had to add another 10 corrections to the next Saturday. Gone were my early Saturday morning rides on my horse. So now, I was dumb and unhappy.

This experience led me to create any excuse I could find to avoid taking a math test in the classroom. If there was a pop quiz, I'd fall suddenly "ill" and you know what? Nine times out of 10, my trick worked. Later, I would study with my classmates and get their help in understanding the problems so I'd have the right answers before my "makeup test."

When I graduated high school, surprisingly, I wanted to go on to college, but did not feel academically equipped to succeed at least that is what I was led to believe. My parents however, believed that college education for women was only good for finding a husband and they wanted me to go to finishing school instead.

My dream was to go to France, live with a French family, become fluent in the language and attend university in Grenoble. I wanted something different and the only reason I believe they heard my voice this time was because my mother had lived in France along with her sister, brother and her mother for a time after her father died.

So things got better for "Dumb" Sallie. I found a family of six boys—worlds apart from my family of five girls—and immersed myself in their culture, in all the art I could find and in skiing the Alps. I spoke fluent French, did my homework in French and even dreamed in French. I traveled everywhere I could, experiencing every piece of sculpture, every masterpiece and every avenue available to me.

When I returned home after my time abroad, I had to face the dreaded question: "What's next?" This time, my parents' desire for me to go to finishing school won over. I thought my life was over and rebelled in kind: you want me to wear gloves and stockings to school? No way! It was a very long year.

When I started my company, The Rocking Horse, in 1976, I had to deal with my dreaded enemy Math again. I was responsible for doing the books, taxes etc...so math and I had to make amends. Because I was invested in making this new venture work, I had to step up to the plate and BELIEVE I could handle this business math. In other words, I had to change the stripes I was wearing. I no longer feared math and am convinced that the calculator was invented just for my purposes, and after all, God gave me 10 fingers, right?

How was I able to do that? Remember, I saw myself as not smart, not quick to learn and not articulate. In order to change that belief about myself, I had to WANT to change it. The financial and emotional investment I had in The Rocking Horse motivated me to do that. I had a choice – I could either hide under the cloak of "dumbness" or change the attire. I decided I needed to change the attire (literally my company designed and manufactured outerwear).

Exercise: Mining for Gold

1. Where do you hear your inner voice demeaning you?
2. What does it sound like?
3. What do you know about yourself to be positive and true?
4. Write down your values (e.g. honesty, kindness, compassion).
5. Where do you see your positive and true beliefs show up in your life? What about your values?

Tip: If you're not sure what your strengths are, I highly recommend taking the Values in Action Survey (VIA): Your 24 Signature Strengths designed by Martin Seligman and available online at www.viacharacter.org/VIASurvey/tabid/55/Default.aspx

"The belief that becomes truth for me...is that which allows me the best use of my strength, the best means of putting my virtues into action."

Andre Gide, The Counterfeiters

Chapter 7
Self-Care Tools: Taking Care Of Number One

"In order to make the best use of your time, in order to do twice as much in half the time, you must take time for "I" and "me." You must make time to recharge and be rejuvenated."

Amy Jones

TOOL #1
HOW TO TELL IF YOU'RE NEGLECTING YOURSELF

"Self-love, is not so vile a sin as self-neglecting."

William Shakespeare

There are many medical definitions of self care on the Web—some holistic in nature, some not—but the common thread among them is looking at self care in terms of the decisions we make and activities we engage in that improve or restore our physical health as well as our mental and emotional well-being. The intention is to heal whatever conditions we may be dealing with, but more importantly, to reduce our stress load to minimize the risk of getting sick and maximize our ability to show up for others.

This is especially important when our already-busy lives include caring for aging parents or a sick child or spouse. As many of you know, it's tough being a caregiver. Even in the best of times it can feel like you are swimming against the tide, not able to get enough air or rest of any kind. That's why it's critical to reach out to others and ask for support **before** you get completely overwhelmed. That is good self care!

If we wait too long to seek this support, we can find ourselves sinking to the bottom of the ocean. And what happens then? We notice that we're filling up with resentment, anger and frustration—at least I do. My pattern is to grow resentful, then grow silent. The people around me can sense my edginess and I get prickly.

This pattern hasn't been easy for me to break for, as I like to say, I have a master's degree in coming to the aid of others, but failed the course in asking for help for myself.

So what does it look and feel like when you're neglecting yourself and barely keeping your head above the water?

- Your body might begin to tense up.

- You become irritable.
- You feel the weight of the world on your shoulders.
- Your emotions are right under the surface of your skin.
- You could cry at any moment or want to.
- You want to runaway to get away from it all.
- You feel exhausted.
- The simplest errand or task is overwhelming.
- You begin to talk to yourself, sputtering discontent and negativity.
- You're short-tempered and yell at things beyond your control.

If you find yourself experiencing any of the symptoms above, now is the time to reach out and get the support you need so you can be a caregiver to yourself. And yes, I've heard all the excuses why you can't:

- No one can do it better than me.
- If I ask them to do it, I will just have to redo it.
- If they help me, then I will have to do something for them.
- I don't want to burden them.
- They have busy lives too.
- I don't want to appear weak.
- Everyone thinks I have it together.
- I'm embarrassed to ask.
- I should be able to do it all (my personal favorite).

Want to know something? I've used some of these excuses too, but my situation didn't change. I still needed help, I was still feeling overwhelmed and I still couldn't get out of my own way.

When I work with clients whose lives are so cluttered they're not taking care of themselves, I always ask, "Why is it important for you to do it all?"

Then, the flood gates open and a much deeper learning experience begins. Some clients feel that they literally don't have support to draw on from family or friends. They feel alone or they feel they're only surrounded by people who need something from them. Other clients have never given a thought to what self care means—they've never given it to themselves and always continue to give to others, thus leaving themselves out of the equation. And finally, we get to experience what happens if they take the risk to ask for help and are met with disappointment when the answer is "NO."

What's interesting is that people who have an enormously hard time asking for help are usually the same people who are first on the scene when someone else asks for their support. A key component of practicing self care is learning what you can do to change that habit.

Exercise: What Do You Need Help With?

Write down what it is that you have trouble asking for. Is it asking for participation around the house? Delegating work at the office? What is it for you?

TOOL #2

HOW TO ASK FOR HELP

> *"The strong individual is the one who asks for help when he needs it. Whether he has an abscess on his knee or in his soul."*

Rona Barrett

Whenever we seek to change any habit, it's best to start by taking small steps. I remember distinctly that time in my life when I had three children under the age of 10, I was working part-time volunteering at three different schools, driving three different car pools, attending their various outside activities. I was spent. Exhausted. There was never time for me and I wanted and needed to create that time.

How did I do that? I wrote down everything I didn't want to do…clearly understanding what was age appropriate for my children to be able to handle or what I could delegate to another adult.

If you have a family, start by making a list of things you need help with. For example, household chores:

- Taking out the trash
- Setting the table
- Cooking
- Shopping and errands
- Laundry
- Getting the mail
- Dishes and other cleaning

Keep this list going until you run out of ideas.

If you live by yourself and need help the same method applies. Reach out to a friend, a neighbor, a co-worker you're close with or a member of your church. Your doctor can point you toward resources and support groups and don't forget that your local librarian can help you research what you need.

Once I made my own list, then I had to choose the one thing I wanted off my plate the most. LAUNDRY! And so we had a family meeting. I stated that I was feeling exhausted, I needed more help around the house, I wanted people to be more responsible and I needed to use the time I freed up to do something for myself.

I want to emphasize here that how something is communicated makes or breaks the conversation. What do you think would have happened if I'd ranted and raved, saying things like:

"No one around here pulls their weight!"

"Corey, you are lazy and don't do x, y, z..."

"Sarah, you never pick up after yourself, leave your toys everywhere, and I am left to pick them up each night."

"Conway, you come home from work and are tired. I am too at the end of the day...why can't you do ..."

I'll tell you what would have happened: I would have come across as a complainer, a bully and everyone around me would have reacted defensively. Even if I were feeling angry and resentful, communicating in that way would have been a no-win and so much for the meeting!

So what did I do? I began by saying:

"I wanted to have this meeting so each of you would hear what I am feeling. There is a lot to do to care for all of you children, take care of a house, get you all to school and your activities as well as run a business part-time.

I am finding myself really tired at the end of the day and would like to have just a little time just for me to do something I like to do. I have made a list of all the things I believe you could help me out with. So I am going to ask if each one of you would be willing to help me out here by choosing a chore you would be willing to do."

Tip: Allowing someone to CHOOSE which job they want to do is half the battle, for they have already bought into the process. Make the list age appropriate if that's applicable to your situation.

Each child chose a chore. The oldest Corey, age 10, did his own laundry; Sarah, age 7, helped by setting the table; and Taylor, age 4, fed the dog.

Many times all you need is a smiling face, someone to listen, someone to encourage, someone to care, someone to be present in the moment or to give you a hug. But, if you need more...ASK for it. In learning to take better care of yourself, it is important to know what you need.

Practice by asking one person who you believe would never say "no." It is important to know that asking will get better the more it is practiced. Keeping things bottled up can bring upon "dis-ease." You owe it to yourself and others to start where you stand by taking small steps to create your self care. And if you model this behavior, you will teach those around you that self care is important and vital to their own health.

Exercise: Clearing Space on Your Plate

- Make a list of jobs or chores you wish to remove from your plate.
- Make sure they are all age appropriate.
- Have your family members CHOOSE which jobs they wish to do.

Now it is your turn...

And you have a job too!!! CHOOSE one person who you believe will not say "no" to you when you ask for help. Now ask them to do something for you...(come on you can do this!) be brave, just ask!

Start with just something small. You are practicing here.

TOOL #3
GETTING OUT OF YOUR OWN WAY

"Take a look at your life. Is there any time in your day for you?"

Julie Fisher-McGarry

When you've created a pattern where you do everything and give everything all the time, it can feel strange at first to accept the help you're getting. You may still feel like you should be able to do it all or that things aren't getting done the way they should be. These feelings—and what we do with them—are part of the pattern.

I taught my son Corey how to use the washing machine, how much detergent to use, how to clean out the lint collector and sort the clothes. Using bleach was a "learning" experience to say the least, but the first thing you need to remember when you give up an item on your to-do list is letting go of the results or outcome!

Yes, Corey's clothes sometimes looked tie-dyed, but it only happened a few times. And yes, when the drawers were empty, he had to tackle the mountain of laundry, but it also taught him to keep up with things once he realized how much time laundry took away from his play when he put it off.

I can hear some of you saying the child's complaining of the lack of clothes would push you into doing it for them. But what does that teach them? The power of complaining and how to manipulate!

So what if Sarah set the table incorrectly, if the forks were on the right and the knife and spoon were on the left? So be it! If I wanted to create time to take care of myself, I had to give up my perfectionist ways. Sarah learned how to set the table correctly over time, but while she was first learning, it was more effective to thank her for her willingness to help than correct her mistakes. And, yup, our dog may have been eating his food off the floor once in a while instead of out of his dog dish, but praising my four-year-old for helping was worth its weight in gold (and the spillage on the floor).

What would it feel like to be able to take something off your plate? Start small and watch your self-esteem rise.

Exercise: What Does Getting Help Feel Like?

Refer to the exercise in Tool #3 to get you started. Write in a journal the feelings experienced when taking something off your plate.

- What was that like for you?
- What was the struggle?
- What was the win?
- What was the learning moment?

TOOL #4

CREATING A SELF-CARE PLAN

"Create a definite plan for carrying out your desire and begin at once, whether you are ready or not, to put this plan into action."

Napoleon Hill

So now you've identified what you need help with, asked for the support you need and are learning to let go of the results so you can focus on yourself. What are you supposed to do with that extra time?

Look to activities and pastimes that you know bring joy into your life or relax you. Even if I only had an extra 15 minutes, I would use that time to flip through a catalog while sitting on my screened-in porch, to take a short walk, to do a little work in the garden. Sometimes I'd phone a dear friend. If I had more time, I'd schedule a massage! The point is, it didn't matter so much what I was doing, but that it was MY time when all the other errands and demands of me were put aside. And it felt great!

Many times we go through life forgetting to look up or down; to the right or left...we are missing what life has to show us. I wrote about this last year on my blog:

WHAT ARE YOU MISSING?

You are busy everyday. The world goes on, never stopping to breathe. Do you find yourself on a treadmill, literally or figuratively? Many do. So how do you slow down? Do you even slow down on your vacation?

Here are a couple of suggestions to slow down. Think about one thing you wish to do, but start small: get a massage, take a walk, sit and read or spend 15 minutes of quiet time by yourself with a cup of tea. In order to keep yourself fueled, you have to revitalize yourself. If you can't read a whole book in a week... read one chapter! Make the commitment to yourself.

I am on vacation right now and am replenishing myself in nature. Yesterday I took a four-mile walk along the Snake River, seeing moose and soaking up the mountain air. I might have missed the most amazing sight, but I was able to pay attention long enough to hear a voice inside tell me to look up. There above me was the most beautiful bald eagle.

It must have been 15 feet above my head perched on the aspen branch. I stopped, camera out, clicked away...then, I stood and spoke to it. It just stared at me; yellow beak bent low in my direction probably sizing me up as if I were to be his next snack. I was taken by its curiosity of me. Our eyes fixed on each other, but the eagle never expanded its wings, content to be "hangin' out" by the banks of the river.

I continued on with my walk and noticed that just by stopping and really experiencing that encounter, my heart was filled with joy. When I met up with other people out for a walk on the path, I told them about the eagle and watched their eyes light up with excitement. I had filled my soul with the wonderment of nature.

Now some people would not feel the same as I did, and that is perfectly okay. Find something to do, what interests you, and just do it. When you are emotionally refueled, you are emotionally available to others. So what's missing? And how are you going to refuel?

Here's a list of suggestions to rekindle your relationship with yourself:

- Go to the movies by yourself or with a friend.
- Buy flowers for yourself.
- Hire a sitter and plan a date night.
- Hire a sitter and go out by yourself.
- Head to the beach or lake.
- Go to the mountains.
- Have a cup of coffee at your favorite place.
- Buy a box of chocolates.
- Doodle.
- Write in your journal.

Below are some "AH-HA" moment stories from my clients that occurred while they were learning to take better care of themselves:

"Erin"

"But the biggest (challenge for me) would be to schedule "me" time, to value myself that way, and to begin the process of self-care, with positive results beginning upon and then so doing. Journaling, too! I did quite a bit of both over the summer and then, as if one season was supposed to be enough, fall was a giant step backwards. I chuckle now to think that there would be an end point to self-care!"

"Susan"

"I have been able to maintain some sense of boundaries during this tumultuous year... At some point, you realize that one can do only so much for even those closest to you. My parents had many good years, in which they enjoyed their senior lunches at various places, puttered, made their calls, did their errands, and were back in time to rest and avoid the horrible traffic that plagues us...Well, so it goes for all of us at some point.

I have come to understand that one really has to allow enough time for yourself - to rest, to be with friends, to make fun time with family, to simply balance out the challenges that we all face. But it will help tremendously to hear positive words and suggestions. I hope to take daily walks that will boost my energy."

Exercise: Getting to Know You

- Write down what it is you will do to rekindle that relationship with yourself.
- Make a list of your interests.
- What brings a smile to your face?
- What makes you laugh?

TOOL #5

BEING KIND TO YOURSELF

"There is only one corner of the universe you can be certain of improving, and that's your own self."

Aldous Huxley

Self care also means forgiving yourself for your failures. Don't beat yourself up! You know I spoke of that perpetual "to-do" list...well don't beat yourself up if you haven't finished it. Congratulate yourself for the items you got done. That is self-care!

As long as you are taking care of the necessary things that are getting done, you don't have to worry about checking off every single item.

Life has a beat of its own; there will be times when it will throw you a curve. It will change your priorities and your level of energy. You might find you are in a relationship that is not healthy for you, midway through a project that's too long to finish and you're drained, or maybe just plain unmotivated to do anything. Don't despair; life is like a rollercoaster…there are major ups and downs. It is important to buckle your seatbelt and give yourself the room to ride whatever it is.

It serves no purpose to beat yourself up; this only diminishes your self-confidence. Where do we find this showing up in our lives? Here's a sprinkling: over-committing, mismanaging our time, procrastination, lack of follow through, perfectionism, guilt, and not thinking before we speak, to name a few.

In order for you to avoid these pitfalls, do a self-assessment and try to identify what event or other trigger led you to abandon yourself. What did you learn from it? Now, forgive yourself for it and start over with a clear sense of what you'll do differently when you're tempted to leave yourself off your own list.

Exercise: Forgive Yourself

Write down what you believe caused you to abandon yourself and your self care.

Now write down "**I** forgive myself, I **forgive** myself, I forgive **myself**." Repeat it several times a day with the emphasis on each bolded word.

TOOL #6
HOW TO NURTURE YOURSELF

"Guard your own spare moments. They are like uncut diamonds."

Ralph Waldo Emerson

Definitions of nurturing:

- Foster: help develop, help grow; "nurture his talents"
- Rear: bring up; "raise a family;" "bring up children"
- Raising: the properties acquired as a consequence of the way you were treated as a child
- Nourish: provide with nourishment; "We sustained ourselves on bread and water;" "This kind of food is not nourishing for young children"
- Breeding: helping someone grow up to be an accepted member of the community; "They debated whether nature or nurture was more important"

- The act of nourishing or nursing; tender care; education; training; That which nourishes; food; diet; the environmental influences that contribute to the development of an individual; see also nature; to nourish or nurse en.wiktionary.org/wiki/nurture

In reading through these definitions, I'm struck by the different ways we can look at nurturing. Self care is also a form of nurturing—the nurturing of one's self—and the words I use when I talk about it include terms like "foster (to grow within), "nourish" (not only in food, but in spirit), "tender care" (being kind to ourselves) and "protection" (in the sense of setting boundaries).

When we are truly nurturing ourselves, we foster or learn how to tap more deeply into this innate talent. For example, if you have a particular skill or activity you excel in, how do you continue to nurture that in yourself? By practicing, studying or even working with a coach or mentor.

The important thing to remember is somewhere in your soul you love to do what you do best—we all do. Don't ever leave that by the wayside—especially when times are tough—it's what brings out the best in you. It nurtures your soul, brings you confidence and gives you joy.

We nurture, or nourish ourselves, not only through what we eat, how we exercise or the quality of our rest, but also through heartfelt experiences. Some eat to "nurture what hurts." I know I have in the past. We look to our comfort foods. Pasta is my most favorite, followed up with a long piece of French bread. I've been known in times of stress to eat an entire baguette on the way home from the market.

This isn't so much self-nurturing as it is looking for instant gratification. Unfortunately, it also adds pounds to my body, delivers more starch into my body that I don't need and does nothing to erase the stress in the long run!

Clearly, this is a negative way of caring for myself. I know it's not healthy for my body or my spirit, but in those moments....aahhhh....it's a quick fix. At times like these, I take a step back and ask myself, "What is it that nourishes you?"

The answer is rarely spaghetti. It's more apt to be working in the garden, tending to the plants and flowers, scratching in the dirt; looking at art or reading an inspirational book; or taking a walk down a wooded path, being ever so curious about what I see around me with every step; playing or walking with our Alaskan Malamute Kodi or having deep conversations with my husband; being quiet, being in the present moment, and taking time for me, perhaps by listening to Andre Boccelli or Les Miserable and other music that touches my soul.

As you can see, it's not enough sometimes to just "take care" of ourselves with that extra helping of noodles. We need to take "tender care" of ourselves. For if we do not do it, who will? It is our responsibility to look after our own welfare.

Exercise: How to Take Tender Care of Yourself

Use your journal or a pad of paper to explore the following:

- What does tender care mean to you?
- Does it mean you follow a spiritual path, does it mean you surround yourself with only positive thinking people?
- Does it mean you will be more gentle with yourself? What would that look like? What happens if you let go of judging others? Does that free up energy to nurture yourself? Remember, when you judge others, you are also judging yourself.
- How can you be kinder to yourself and let go of self-judgment?

One of the key components of self care and nurturing is learning how to protect ourselves. By that I mean setting boundaries, which isn't easy for everyone and takes some practice, especially for people-pleasers.

When you think about protecting yourself, you might decide to spend more time with people who lift you up, make you laugh and encourage you. Do not EVER allow anyone to bully, verbally or physically abuse you. This will never nourish you.

The saying, "you can pick your friends but you can't pick your family" rings true. Even if you find you are not the best friends with your brother-in-law, Aunt Edna or your cousin, guess what, you don't have to be! If they don't give you the support and love you need, there are others who do and will. Seek them out.

Exercise: Learning to Nurture Yourself

So what can you do? Write down all the ways that you can nurture yourself. The following questions may help you make your list.

- How can you foster your growth?
- What nourishes you and why?

- When did you last feel joy?
- What does this tell you about yourself?
- Where can you begin to set boundaries so you have more room in your life for self care?

Here are some things to try so you can learn more about what nourishes you: practice deep breathing several times a day, get an acupressure treatment, mediate or pray, get a massage, write in your journal, spend time in nature, spend time for reflection, cherish those around you, surround yourself with kind and loving people, play, sing, read, be inspired, be open to what the Universe has to offer, be open-minded and remember to exercise.

TOOL #7

RECOGNIZING A SELF-CARE EMERGENCY

"Taking time for yourself should never be seen as a burden. Not on you, and not on anyone else."

Elizabeth Franklin

Did you know that families are coming back together in ways the United States has not seen in 50 years? According to a recent Pew Research Center analysis of Census data, as of 2008, a record 49 million Americans (16.1%) lived in a family household inhabiting two adult generations of one kind or another and the trend is rising higher even today.

"As we have seen, children take longer to leave home, grandparents care for grandchildren and while parents work and adult children help care for their aging parents. Since bottoming out in 1980, the trend has risen to a 50-year high because more people need help after losing their jobs, filing for bankruptcy, facing foreclosure or having their savings wiped out," explains Tim Grant of the Pittsburgh Post-Gazette.

The Pew Research Center states that this trend is going to accelerate as the house market falls, job uncertainty continues, graduates from college return home, and the cost of nursing homes becomes prohibited. Maybe this is suppose to happen for all of us to wake up and see what our fathers and forefathers have known for centuries: multigenerational family living could very well be our roots.

A lot of us now, are managing our own lives, while, to some extent, caring for our adult children and our parents who may be ailing or ill and need our support. We're being pulled at both ends and have no idea how to play to the middle, which is where we reside.

In 1999 my husband and I were remodeling our kitchen. I had just finished a meeting with the contractor when the telephone rang. It was my sister, Gretchen, calling to give me the update of our father who had been suffering with congestive heart failure and emphysema.

The entire year had been particularly hard—my kids were young, the stress and worry over my father manifested as an onslaught of hives on my body, and to top it off, we were living in the mess of mid-construction. I was exhausted, to say the least, but harder than that was the push-pull I felt between my own family's needs and the desire to be there for my father.

What do you think happened to me? I began to grow forgetful, my nutrition was out of whack with cravings for pasta and other carbohydrates and I was forever taking a nap whenever I could fit one in.

Additionally, I felt guilty over how many of my kids' activities I was missing and my temper was short. I was fortunate that my husband stepped up to the plate and could be there physically and emotionally to help with dinner, homework, carpools and bedtimes. On the other hand he really just HAD to show up—I was completely unavailable in almost every way.

Then there was the one time when I drove down to New Bedford to visit my father in the hospital. I pulled into Dunkin' Donuts to get a cup of coffee and started getting annoyed that the drive thru wasn't responding after I'd ordered. As it turned out, I was so out of my wits that I'd been giving my order to the trash bin that stood BEFORE the order microphone. To this day, it's a running joke in my house and especially with my sisters.

Here are some signs to watch out for (in yourself or in others) that indicate you're in need of some emergency self care:

- Are you/they continually getting ill?
- Are you/they sleep deprived?
- Are you/they growing forgetful?
- Are you/they not eating enough during the day?
- Are you/they feeling down, showing signs of depression or have difficulty getting out of bed?
- Do you/they feel alone or isolated?
- Are you/they constantly doubting your/their decisions and seeking reassurance?
- Are you/they becoming abrupt, short-tempered, and angry?

- Are you/they feeling guilty for having missed their children's activities, birthdays, vacations, and for not being present?

Exercise: Taking Care in Tough Times

Next, I want you to spend a few moments answering the following questions which will get you ready to put your self-care into motion:

- What are you experiencing now that is burdensome?
- What are things you could do to take care of your self?
- Who are those around you who could help?
- What action will you take to relieve some of this stress?

I want to end this chapter with a very personal letter I wrote to my father on November 11, 2000.

"Dearest Dup,

Funny, I sit here beside you holding your hand. What a smooth soft hand it is. You wake occasionally and pop open those wide blue eyes, trying to focus, looking a bit confused and surprised. I rub your arm and tell you it is 'Lulie.' You hum your little hum, I return the compliment; I have heard that same pitch so many times before. It reminds me of a lion cub nuzzling up to its mother.

I do not feel sad sitting here beside you. I feel tremendously privileged to be able to care for you. You have given us A GIFT—a wonderful gift! Your generation may call it a burden, but your daughters don't feel that way. How more intimate is a moment like this!

At times you speak of having seen your parents and heard their voices, of seeing Uncle John and George. Where do you travel when you are so deep in sleep? You say you are at sea or in the sky. You speak of light. You say how peaceful and wonderful it is. I would hope nothing less for you.

How soft your skin is—did I tell you that we all marvel over your most meticulously manicured nails? You are the only male on earth that sleeps with his nail clippers. I use mine for my toes, the kids pop blisters with theirs.

There has not been a day that I have not thought of the smell of the barn at Petticoat Hill, the horses, the hayloft, saddle soap, the mice in the grain bins, our morning rides and the constant shoveling out of the stalls.

Did I tell you how much that meant to me? THE WORLD!!! Though I will blame you for my fear of ladders and heights. Your sick sense of humor would sometimes kick in. You would shake the wooden ladder as I tried to come down from the loft. The harder I held on for dear life, the more you shook it. It was better to exit by jumping into the newly piled hay below. The crossness in your voice over my action was a better consequence. Yes, I will loosen up the hay. God forbid, I flattened it.

I can still smell the coffee and the boiling of eggs in the dim light in the kitchen in Holden. The Proutys were picking us up early to go skiing. The rest of the house snug under their covers. Donning the latest stretch pants, and what I thought was the most beautiful parka at that moment, we piled into the station wagon. 'Don't crease the knees was the slogan for the day!'

Do you remember how many fingers of yours bled on those weekends? Let's see, you laced up four pairs of leather ski boots! Gortex was not yet invented. We stayed warm and dry under those blankets, as we advanced to the oncoming chairlift. You would fire up your pipe and off you'd go...from one side to the other, pipe in mouth. Why you were never impaled by it is beyond me, let alone how you never swallowed it.

Then, there were the trips to sea. Cruising to Maine or Long Island. Meeting you across the pond in Ireland and Denmark. Visiting Passat in Germany. She is very much a part of our lives. THEN, the trip out west! Our air conditioning unit, a block of ice hung from the top of the driver's window!! Sleeping arrangements...you and Mom were banned from the bus – your snoring even woke up the wildlife.

My summers were spent cutting and haying the fields, manure fights and seeking employment from you...the original Captain Bligh. Did you know that I still have the contract you created for me? Let me jog your memory. It reads: "Thou shalt not work under the sun in a skimpy bikini, nor listen to that loud music known as rock and roll." That left me boiling under the hot sun completely covered. At 16 years old, believe me, melanoma was the farthest from my mind.

And as I write this, your mouth hangs open wide, your gurgle of a snore is of little notice to me now. I tend to take great pleasure in those noises. It is comforting, familiar and YOU!!!

I shall miss your prankstering, if there is such a word; I hope that those genes are strong and are passed down to the next generation. Lord knows that I have fostered them in our children. How they love to hear stories of Labor Day at the beach. Do you know how much your grandchildren love the beach house? It feels like home to them, a place where all the cousins can be together. A time of family of tradition, of you and Mom...a connectedness. Stories of Holden, of Hazie, of times gone by.

You see we are all a part of what you both created. Five daughters!! I know that you wanted to ship us all out between the ages of 13-18; being the only male was tough. The Estrogen level at an all-time high. But, you got through it. You bought your boy toys and the onslaught of sons-in-law were a great tonic.

Now we talk of hot flashes and menopause. But these are all the stories of the love I have had being with you. Sharing adventures and secrets.

Thank you Dad for allowing me to care for you ....you have given each of us a GIFT!!!

I love you forever, 'til we meet again,

Sallie"

Dad died on December 16, 2000. I said my "goodbyes and bid him smooth sailing" earlier, joyful of having read the letter to him at his bedside prior to his death. You see he knew that I was sharing the letter at his eulogy. Of all the people I wanted to hear my words, it was my father. I was not going to miss that opportunity to tell the person I loved what they meant to me! Even in grief, this was a way for me to NURTURE my soul, to nurture my sadness, to nurture the child in me who cried.

Why is it we tell the people we love what they have meant to us AFTER they are no longer in our lives? Why not tell them before; for you will not have another chance later?

I have no regrets and encourage you all to open up your hearts for life is way too short.

Chapter Eight
Future Tools: Charge!!! Taking Action

"The test of any man lies in action"

Pindar

TOOL #1

DISCOVERING WHAT YOU WANT

"We have what we seek. It is there all the time, and if we give it time it will make itself known to us."

Thomas Merton

At this point in this book, it's my hope that you have a sense of how the three forms of clutter—mental, physical and emotional—interrelate as well as how they affect you and your environment. Whatever kind of clutter you are dealing with, it is imperative for you to decide:

1. What is your goal or vision?
2. What do you wish to come into your life?
3. What do you wish to remove from your mental, physical and emotional clutter?

So what is your vision? What are your goals? Here are just some of the hundreds which I have heard from clients over the years:

- More Laughter
- Peace
- Freedom
- Balance
- Clarity
- Purpose
- Happiness
- Health
- More Compassion
- Volunteer Time
- More Time with Family

- More Time with your Life Partner
- Joy of Working
- Tranquility
- Sense of Accomplishment
- More sleep/rest
- Acceptance
- Kindness to Self

My client "Lee" had a goal and a vision, beginning with de-cluttering four rooms in her house. As we talked more about this and her other goals, I had her write them all down so we had a visual map of them. Here is her summary:

1. *Physical Clutter:*
   a. *De-clutter four rooms in my house*
   b. *Kitchen*
   c. *Master Bedroom*
   d. *Home Office*
   e. *Attic*

2. *Mental Clutter:*
   a. *Use a calendar more effectively*
   b. *Write down each evening what I want to accomplish tomorrow at work*
   c. *Learn to delegate tasks*

3. *Emotional Clutter:*
   a. *Write down a personal goal implementing daily self care*
   b. *Spend more time with family*
   c. *Explore an exercise routine*

As we continued our session together, I had Lee go into more detail about each of these goals, but for brevity's sake, I've chosen one of them to show you step by step how she implemented the SMART goals system to make it happen.

Sallie: "What is it you wish to see (or what is your vision/goal) when the kitchen is done?"

Lee: "A cleaner space, plants around the windows, space utilized better, mail off the counters, kitchen cabinets and drawers organized

Sallie: "What does it give you (or what will you have) when this task is completed?"

Lee: "Huge satisfaction, less stress, a sense of order."

Using the SMART goals system, here's how Lee broke the task of de-cluttering the kitchen into smaller steps.

TOOL #2

S is for SIMPLE AND SPECIFIC:

"Determine what specific goal you want to achieve. Then dedicate yourself to its attainment with unswerving singleness of purpose, the trenchant zeal of a crusader."

Paul J. Meyer

When you outline your goals and/or identify a project you're going to take on, it's imperative that you make sure the tasks you define are SIMPLE. By that I mean, the tasks by themselves aren't overwhelming.

Next, you need to be SPECIFIC about what you want to get done. "Cleaning out the pantry" is too big, too vague. You need to get detailed and always keep your vision or outcome for the project in mind.

Sallie: "Lee, make a detailed list of the simple tasks that need to be done to complete this, always keeping your focus on the finished product...your vision."

Lee: "I am going to write a list of areas of the kitchen I wish to tackle and what I want within that."

1. *Cabinets: clean them all out, wash them down, discard old mugs, chipped or broken china or glassware, throw out dated cans boxes, spices.*

2. *Drawers: clean them all out, wash them down, organize space and placement of utensils, silverware, pots and pans.*

3. *Counters: de-clutter all mail, catalogs, magazines, find place for kids book bags.*

4. *Windowsill: add color to the windowsill, add more green plants (ivy).*

Notice that Lee was very specific about what she wanted to get done within each of her tasks, even going so far as to choose ivy plants for her windowsill.

TOOL #3

M is for MEASUREABLE

"Measure what is measurable, and make measurable what is not so."

Galileo Galilei

Next, you want to make sure the tasks you've defined for yourself are measurable. Review your list of tasks and ask yourself:

- Is this a task that can be measured?
- How long will this task take me?
- How will I feel when I complete this task?
- Do I need to break this task down further?
- Does this task support my overall vision or desired outcome?

Here's how Lee measured her kitchen de-cluttering tasks:

Cabinets

- *Clean them all out: allow ½-hour per cabinet*
- *Wash them down: allow five minutes per cabinet*
- *Discard old mugs, chipped or broken china or glassware: allow ½-hour to sort*
- *Throw out dated cans boxes, spices, inspect expiration dates, allow 45 minutes to sort*

Drawers

- *Clean them all out: allow one hour for all drawers*
- *Wash them out: allow 45 minutes for all drawers*
- *Organize utensils, flatware, pots and pans: allow two hours*

Counters

- *De-clutter all mail: allow 15 minutes*
- *Sort catalogs and magazines: allow 10 minutes*
- *Find place for kids' book bags, relocate: allow 10 minutes*

Windowsill

- *Add color to the windowsill (visit florist): 10 minutes*
- *Add more green plants (visit florist): 10 minutes*

Notice how Lee approximated the time she'd need to complete each task. This helps her plan her time and, as she completes these smaller goals, contributes to her vision for a cleaner, more organized and less stressful space.

TOOL #4

A is for ATTAINABLE:

"Persist and persevere, and you will find most things that are attainable, possible."

Lord Chesterfield

Lee and I both had confidence that she could de-clutter her kitchen. She broke large tasks down into smaller ones and estimated the amount of time each task would take, but we needed to make sure these tasks were attainable. In other words, Lee needed to be able to keep herself on course and motivated to continue.

In looking at your own goals and tasks, ask yourself:

- Can this task/goal be attained? Hint: the answer is always YES.
- How will I get it done?
- What do I need to do to stay on course and motivate myself?
- How can I limit my self-doubt and stay positive?

For Lee, the answer was easy. When she set forth to complete her tasks, she needed to limit distractions—no cell phone, no texting, no stopping for a snack—and commit to making these tasks happen.

I asked Lee if she liked to work in silence or with background noise and/or music. Lee said she liked to work to music, so I suggested she play her favorite CD and work until that CD has ended.

Then, we talked about how she'd stay motivated. Lee felt that if she could devote a little time each day to these tasks, she'd feel a tremendous amount of accomplishment. Here's an example of how she did that.

We already knew that she needed to de-clutter her cabinets and it would take about a half-an-hour per cabinet to empty the contents and put them in boxes, sort through the contents and decide what to keep, and segregate items for disposal or donation to the food pantry.

To make it attainable and keep her motivated, she planned to play her favorite music and limit her de-cluttering session to three cabinets a day/

night. It sounded like a great plan, but the next step was to determine if it was realistic for Lee.

TOOL #5

R is for REALISTIC

"I always like to look on the optimistic side of life, but I am realistic enough to know that life is a complex matter."

Walt Disney

When we put a plan in place to achieve our goals, it's easy to either underestimate or overestimate what we can get done and when. This is why it's important to be honest with yourself about whether the plan you put into place is realistic or not. In Lee's case, she wanted to tackle three cabinets a day/night until this part of the kitchen was done.

Sallie: "Lee, I see that you are making it a goal to do three cabinets each night. Is this realistic?"

Lee: "Well actually, I have a dinner meeting one night this week, so, yikes, I can't do three every night as I thought. I have failed already!"

Sallie: "Failed? Never! You just realized that your goal for doing three cabinets each night for three consecutive nights might have been unrealistic. Life does get in the way of our routine and goals, so what might work for you if it were not every night?"

Lee: "Could I do one cabinet after my dinner meeting?"

Sallie: "Congratulations, instead of feeling you had failed, you came up with a compromise with yourself that keeps you on plan."

So when you look at your own tasks and goals, be sure to ask yourself:

- Is my plan realistic?
- Am I asking too much (or too little) of myself?
- Can I really accomplish this in the time I've allotted for myself?
- If not, what can I do to chunk these tasks out even further to make it realistic?

Lee felt much better knowing she could "be a bit kinder to herself" and allow this process to ebb and flow with the reality of her life. Sometimes we overestimate what can be done by underestimating the time needed to complete the tasks. Remember, there is no set guideline as to how long it should take a person to do a task—it's about you and your schedule. Some times you might whip right through goals and other times you may need to slow down and be more methodical. It doesn't matter: THIS IS NOT A RACE!

TOOL #6

T is for TIME-ORIENTED

"There are only two mistakes one can make along the road to truth; not going all the way, and not starting."

Buddha

Last, but not least, you'll need to find a way to make yourself accountable for completing your goals—ways to stay on track and make your process time-oriented. The big questions to answer here are:

- When are you going to do the task?
- Are you going to make excuses not to do it?
- What complaints will come to the surface when it's time to get to work?
- How will you deal with procrastination and all the other excuses that come to mind?

When I asked Lee these questions, her answer was excellent, Lee said:

"I'm actually going to use this as an opportunity to practice one of my mental clutter goals which is to use my calendar more effectively. I'm going to block off specific days and times to work on this project. To start, I'll schedule at least three nights a week, using the timeframes I allotted for each task, whether it's 10 minutes or two hours."

Notice: Lee made it a point to be accountable to herself, no one else. If you need to have a friend or family member hold you accountable go ahead and ask them. Beware: many times they cut you too much slack! Remember though, that making things happen must absolutely mean that you will be specific about the time(s) when this will be accomplished.

Putting It All Together

Making the task SIMPLE/ SPECIFIC, MEASUREABLE, ATTAINABLE, REALISTIC and TIME-ORIENTED is the key to success. If your tasks still look overwhelming, divide them further.

I want to make something crystal clear here. I am not talking about climbing Mt. Everest on the first attempt.

What I am talking about is having the gear in place and all the necessary tools to serve you as you begin the climb. Plan how you will complete the task, break it down, do what you can because life does and can get in the way. Accept those struggles as learning moments, not failures! Give yourself a chance; then, with every step, you will be successful.

As you move through your own process, remember:

1. You're wanting to change!
2. You're making or setting your goals.
3. You're showing up for yourself, doing the work.
4. You're being accountable.

Putting all of this together, let's look at Lee's SMART goals strategy for de-cluttering her kitchen cabinets:

SIMPLE AND SPECIFIC

Cabinets

- Clean them all out
- Wash them down
- Discard old mugs, chipped or broken china or glassware
- Throw out dated cans boxes, spices, inspect expiration dates

MEASUREABLE

Cabinets

- Clean them all out: allow ½-hour per cabinet
- Wash them down: allow 5 minutes per cabinet
- Discard old mugs, chipped or broken china or glassware: allow ½-hour to sort
- Throw out dated cans boxes, spices, inspect expiration dates, allow 45 minutes to sort

ATTAINABLE

Cabinets

- Plan to do three cabinets each night
- Limit distractions (no cell phone, no texting, no stopping for snacks)
- Play favorite music in background to stay motivated

REALISTIC

Cabinets

- Rearranged her plans to accommodate her dinner meeting
- Practice kindness to self by allowing herself flexibility in scheduling

TIME-ORIENTED

Cabinets

- Blocked off specific days/times on her calendar to de-clutter her cabinets
- Made herself accountable by using her calendar

So how did Lee do with her SMART goals? Throughout her process, she wrote often to update me on her progress and shared her victories.

Physical Clutter Victory:

"I'm taking at least an hour each day or the length of a CD to tackle something in the kitchen... and then plan out my next couple weeks. Today it was a couple drawers in my kitchen; the other day the boxes in my bedroom closet. The other evening I did my desk drawers. Then I spent some time on one section of my attic that had boxes containing who knows what."

Emotional Clutter Victory:

"I have also scheduled time for myself to have a massage once a week. Part of my emotional clutter....and self-care. Instead of just letting it go, I make four months of appointments in a row before I leave their offices."

Mental Clutter Victory:

"I wanted you to know that I was working on a huge power-point presentation the other day in the office, had to go out of town unexpectedly, so I asked another colleague to finish the project. Sallie, I delegated!!!! Learning comes in tiny steps... another one from my mental clutter."

Exercise: Start Where You Stand

1. Write down what it is you want to come into your life.
2. What do you want to remove from your mental clutter?
3. What do you want to remove from your physical clutter?
4. What do you want to remove from your emotional clutter?

Sit with these answers and continue to add or delete from it during the course of a week. Write down why it is important to remove these pieces of clutter from your life. Remember when you CHOOSE to get rid of something, you CHOOSE to allow something else to appear! If you hold on to everything, there is no room for more positive energy to come forth.

"Action is a great restorer and builder of confidence. Inaction is not only the result, but the cause of fear. Perhaps the action you take will be successful; perhaps different action or adjustments will have to follow. But any action is better than no action at all."

Norman Vincent Peale

Chapter Nine

Practical Tools: Keeping It All Together
For The Holidays

I have taken a chapter from my e-book "CLUTTER FREE AND CLEAR: Take Charge of Your Time and Space! A how-to book to simplify your life." I write specifically about de-cluttering your mental clutter during the Holidays. It is to the point and provides all the mental tools as well as physical tools to make your Holidays stress free. This is a time of year when the to-do list in your mind is on overdrive.

Why does the word HOLIDAY spark fear in some and total joy in others? So what is it about the Holiday that generates the most stress…those December Holidays! Whether it is Christmas or Hanukkah or any other, it is a time when family and friends get together. A time that is shared, a time remembered and a time you want to be the best.

The keys to the success of any holiday are planning and follow-through. Without those, have you found yourself boarding the "runaway bus?" Are you one of those people who went through the motions and, when all was said and done, you were exhausted, spent, and swore you would do it differently next year? But when that next time came around, was anything noticeably different? More importantly, did YOU have fun?

In this Holiday chapter, I will cover the gift list, decorations, supplies, mailing, storage* and preparation. I will help you get organized and take the "f" out of frustration and put it back into "F"un. Sprinkled throughout this chapter are how-to fix situations and tips* for solutions to make it better.

TOOL #1

ORGANIZE

So, are you worried about how you are going to organize all of this? What could be done differently here than what you have done before? Have you wondered how you were ever going to get everything completed on time? Or better yet, "How am I going to pay for all of this?" Well, consider doing what I tell my clients:

 For a list of Sallie's Clutter Tips and her Practical Go-To-Storage Solutions, go to *www.SoSmartOnline.com/Clutter*

"Take one step at a time."

- Make a list of all that needs to be done. This process is called brainstorming. It is a conscious act of writing down on paper all you need to accomplish. Now you are creating a Master Plan. In order for this to be carried out, it will take discipline and preparation.

- Now prioritize the list…is there anything that can wait until another week, two weeks, or even three?

- Take the list and number it in order of what is critical to get done NOW. Is there anything that is extremely urgent?

- Calculate how much time it will take you to complete each particular task.

- Add 15 minutes to give yourself wiggle room for any interruptions.

- Now, here comes the challenge; make an appointment in your calendar with yourself. Yes, you are now going to be accountable for keeping the appointment.

- If you are dreading a particular task, listen to a CD and stop when it is done playing, take a break, stretch, do what works for you, but don't give up.

- Cross off the task when it is completed and REWARD YOURSELF, especially if the task was huge.

Here are some things you might be thinking about as the Holidays rear their heads…Let's think about to whom you wish to be giving. You need to start by making another list.

TOOL #2

THE HOLIDAY LIST

When you sit down to construct your list, this is the recommendation of Ben Hecht of the non-profit lifestyle and personal-finance site www.thebeehive. org. "When making a list of your gift recipients, make three different groups:

- Make a list of family members.
- Friends that would be receiving smaller gifts.
- Friends and family you need not give to."

He states it is very important to know what you are planning to spend per individual (or what you can afford based on your income) and then tally up the total budget. Stick to this and your Holiday debt will not rear its ugly head in the coming months. This will require discipline, but the goal is to give from the heart; it is not to exceed or outdo someone else.

Having come from a large family myself, I want to share with you some of the ideas I have come up with and have done myself. One does not have to buy an expensive gift to show how much someone means to them. See if any of the following could be useful for you.

Consider giving the gift of time:

- Wrap someone's presents for them
- Address and mail holiday cards
- Bring dinner to someone
- Make cookies once a month
- Offer to go and return unwanted presents for a friend
- Make up a gift card, promise any of the following:
  - yard work
  - babysitting
  - cleaning
  - painting
  - tree pruning
  - baking
- Volunteer to help cater at a friend's event
- If you are a techie, give a lesson on the computer

What's your strength, what do you do well, what would your family or friend like?

My husband and I have three grown children. Each one has a particular strength and their presents usually encompass that part of them. Our oldest, Corey, has spent summers as a tree climber and for the Holidays he has given us a gift certificate promising to trim all the dead wood out of our trees. Our daughter, Sarah, has promised to organize all of our photographs and put them into albums. Our third, Taylor, offered to help with the fall and spring yard work, raking and putting down the mulch.

This is indeed a win-win situation, for they are giving of themselves, and their time, and we benefit from them being at home even more. There is nothing I would want more than to have them around, especially since they live out of the New England area. So think about it… giving of your time is priceless.

Give a family present:

If on a budget, consider buying a gift for the entire family. I have done this on numerous occasions. If they are a sports family, think about a night out skating, a sled, a toboggan, a day pass somewhere, or put a basket together with hot cocoa mixes, popcorn, mugs, hand-and-toe warmers and a movie. For food lovers, how about a basket of unusual gourmet delights, oils, sauces, chocolates, cookbooks, or wines; for city slickers, how about take-out twice a month or a delivery of flowers once a month. How about these: A subscription to sports, cuisine, Consumer Report, traveling, or outdoor magazines. You don't have to give a gift to each and every person in the family. There are movie tickets, museum passes, workshops, lessons…think out-of-the-box. It will be Fun.

Giving a group gift:

If you know there is a particular gift someone on your list would like but it is too much for your budget, feel free to ask a family member to go in on buying the present with you, especially when they would be giving to this person as well.

Sometimes two heads are better than one in choosing just the right gift as well as sharing in the cost.

TOOL #3
YOUR HOLIDAY LIST

Has your list of family and friends been scribbled on that piece of paper next to the telephone or near your computer? Has the list been added to or names crossed out? How many lists have you put into your pocket? And you remembered what he/she wanted, written it down, but now can't find it. I truly understand how that happens and know how that once went for me. Have you put so many sticky notes around that you keep repeating yourself?

I want to share with you something passed down to me by my mother. This method of writing down the "gift-giving list" has been a saving grace for me and I have been using it since 1968. It is a method my sisters, even today, tease me about. Let alone what my grown children say!

Which brings me to wanting to share this story about one of my clients:

My client was pretty well organized but found she had little sticky notes plastered all over her kitchen and car. Does this sound familiar to some of you? She was a person who kept things in her head, a virtual filing cabinet, but then could not remember if she had written it down, whether she had bought the object, or sent it. We came up with a solution that worked with her.

Exercise: The Secret to making this really work:

- Get yourself a spiral notebook, one where you can turn the pages easily and write on both sides of the paper. My size has been an 8-inch by 10-inch. (It all depends how much information you want to keep in this notebook.) I tend to go with the larger ones because I don't want to misplace them.

- If you need to buy one, go to any office supply store such as Staples, Office Max; even your CVS, variety store, or local pharmacy carries them. Choose a size that works for you, and then choose the COLOR you love. By choosing something pleasing to look at will make the job of using the notebook even easier.

() **Green Tip:** If you have children and their old school spiral notebooks have not been used up, tear out their old school notes and recycle the paper.

- Take the spiral notebook and label the outside HOLIDAY BOOK. Use a large indelible ink to label this new organizational tool you will never be without.

- Leave the book where you most likely would have it at your fingertips. Mine is either to the right of my phone in the kitchen or on my desk standing up nearest my action file.

- Now get a pencil that has a good eraser and attach it to the notebook. You do not want to use pen! People's minds change and your list of those "to give" to can also change. Crossing things out and rewriting creates visual clutter.

- You'll need to set up at least nine columns on the page.

The 1st column is for the Name of the Family or Friend who will be receiving the gift.

Tip: Write down first and last name.

The 2nd column is for the Gift you know has been asked for which you might give, or it is something that you think is a natural fit with their personality. Remember the expressions, "It looks just like them," "It is their taste," "Oh, they would so love this," or "This is perfect."

Tip: Items and thoughts might change. Be sure to use a pencil.

The 3rd column is for noting the gift that has been Purchased. If the gift has been bought, put a check next to it.

Tip: Record the date when it was purchased.

The 4th column denotes Receipts Saved.

Tip: This is a good idea. It is a good thing to keep all your receipts. Go one step further when you buy a gift and ask the salesperson to include a receipt in a sealed envelope. When giving a gift, I always put the receipt into the sealed envelope and enclose it under the present. That way the recipient can return the gift if it is not to their liking. This will make any returns much easier.

The 5th column records whether or not you have Wrapped the gift.

Tip: I know you must be thinking, "No, I wrap all my gifts on the eve of the holiday." Well, if you do, you are surely going to be stressed. I used to do that, especially when it came to wrapping our childrens' presents or assembling their toys. My husband said the three most dreaded words during the holidays are "Some Assembly Required." He was right!

Think about having a roll of wrapping paper near where you will be storing your gifts. At that time you can record the gift bought in your notebook. Then remove the price tag from the gift, wrap the item, and place a sticky note of the recipient's name on top (include a notation of what is enclosed if you need to). If you have a gift tag, you can affix it and later decorate with a bow or ribbon until you ship or deliver the gift, so, the bow or ribbon is not crushed.

The 6th column denotes where your gift is going to be Stored.

Tip: It is important to have all of your gifts located in one central area. Here are some ideas as to where you can store them: a closet, corner of a dry basement, a dry attic, or base of a cabinet. If you are storing them in a basement or attic, purchase transparent containers (Rubbermaid and Tupperware both make great containers). This ensures the contents will be dry and organized.

Place some inexpensive shelving in larger spaces such as attics or basements.

The 7th column reminds you when to Ship By. Check your local postal services as to when to ship overseas or domestically.

Tip: Remember, the earlier you ship, the less you will pay.

Two weeks before the holidays you will ship your package PRIORITY to make sure it arrives on time. So plan ahead. If you are having the catalog stores send the packages, they will ask you when you want them to be delivered. Make sure you have the correct address and ask for a tracking number. Some delivery services will not accept a P.O. Box, so be prepared to have an alternative address.

If you are sending them priority mail, know you will be spending more but less than the overnight or three-day services.

Having done this for years, and having an extensive family to buy for, I have learned to have everything ready to go out in the mail by the first week in December.

I have tried to calculate my past postage monies spent from the different services, and believe me, I have used them all. Do what is the most convenient for you. You are the only one who knows for sure how you tick and what is going to work. This is supposed to be easy. If you don't mind driving to the post office or you would rather have UPS or another ground carrier come and pick up your packages, do that. MAKE IT SIMPLE.

The 8th column tells you when you Sent your gift.

Tip: It is important to keep all your receipts and tracking information. Place them in an envelope and keep it in your notebook. Mark the date your gift was sent under this heading.

The 9th column tells you when you Deliver/ed your gift.

Tip: This is not a sprint. Fill up your gas tank and place all your gifts to be delivered into an open container/laundry basket or something like that.

() **Green Tip:** Think about your routes; keep them simple. If you have to deliver a gift in one town, deliver the next in same general location. Have a plan. Let's save on gas as well.

NOTE: There may be some of you who might find it easier to have just a sheet of paper inside a binder. Well, fear not; I have supplied you with Tool #4. It has all of the above-mentioned material but laid out in another form. My advice is to make numerous copies of this sheet and keep them all in your binder.

TOOL #4

WORKSHEET #1, HOLIDAY NOTEBOOK

Don't forget to label the outside of the binder: Holiday Book. And remember to keep this binder in a handy place. Have fun!

WORKSHEET #1

HOLIDAY NOTEBOOK Family/Friend Gift List*

*Note: Make or copy a separate sheet for each recipient

Name: _____

Gift Purchased: _____

Date Purchased: _____

Receipt Saved: yes/no _____

Wrapped: yes/no _____

Where Stored: _____

Ship By/How Shipped: _____

Date Sent: _____

Deliver/ed: yes/no _____

Date Delivered: _____

TOOL #5

WHERE IS EVERYTHING?

I have had clients who cannot find whatever they are looking for. When the holidays come you might wonder if you have all the lights you need, extra bulbs, wrapping paper, Scotch tape, and a tree stand rusted out. Does any

 For your own printable Holiday Gift List template, go to *www.SoSmartOnline.com/Clutter*

of that sound familiar to you? Well, I am here to help you organize your supplies for any holiday. When I first ask my clients about their "collection" of holiday supplies, I often want to know where they store it. Some of their answers are: "under my bed," "in the front hall closet," "hidden in the attic," "buried in the basement," or "it is all over the house."

If you could put these items in a place where it is the most convenient for you, where would it be? Where could you put those indoor or outdoor decorations, ornaments, tree stand, outside lights, window candlelights, wrapping paper, bows, etc. Find an area that will work for you. The key here is to have one central location.

I have a cabinet area under a very large bookcase that is specifically used to house those gifts I buy during the year. Yes, a bike won't fit in there; however, I tape a list of items that don't fit in there and remind myself where they are: basement, garage, and attic. If you are storing them in any of those locations, to keep these presents fresh and dust free, buy a Tupperware or Rubbermaid container and place them inside. Make sure you label the top of the container with HOLIDAY GIFTS.

If you will be storing these overhead, a good idea is to mark the side of the container with the words HOLIDAY GIFTS so you will be able to locate them easily without having to lift them to see what is in there. If you want to "hide" your holiday gifts in the basement or attic, make sure the area where you plan to place these supplies is dry. Place items on inexpensive plastic shelves or use wooden shelves for the heavier items.

Tip: If you don't want tiny eyes to see what you have bought, store in a non-transparent container!

I once used a large corrugated box to store my ornaments until I found an ornament container in the catalogs, www.homeimprovement.com and www.solutions.com. Each one had its own compartment. It is great and very sturdy. Again, I have labeled it on the top and on the sides so I know, or someone else knows, exactly what is in it. I put all the children's handmade ornaments on the bottom of this container. Each of theirs is marked with their name or initial and the date made.

Exercise: Create a Tradition

Begin to create a collection for your own children/grandchildren. Buy a container for them, put their name on it, and each year place an ornament in it that has something to do with them. Could be sports related, music, dance, school, be creative. Put their initials on it with the date. I always give one to each of my children and place it in their respective boxes after it has been on our tree. They love to see the collection and recall the memories.

Make sure your ornaments are in a well-protected, crush-proof container. Label the container to spot instantly. Here are some suggestions on where you can find these items on the Internet such as, www.Solutions.com and www.Rubbermaid.com.

TOOL #6

TIME TO DECORATE

Do you ever hear yourself saying, "Where did I put the string of lights? They were here last year?" Oh, don't you love those exclamations, just like the three dreaded words in our house before Christmas were "Some Assembly Required." NOW... First Things First.

Outside Decorations

Let's keep everything again in one place. Make a promise to yourself that you are going to store all your holiday decorations in one place, be it the attic, tool shed, garage, or basement. No more going under the beds, in an overstuffed closet, or behind the boxes of clothes in the attic, if you don't need to.

Again, the best thing is to have a clear container with a label as to its contents. Remember, those items that are broken need to be replaced before they are packed up at the end of the season. Be sure all the strings of lights are untangled when you put them away for the season.

Exercise: Buy Now!

Take advantage of all the sales after the holidays. Buying bulbs, wrapping paper, ribbons, bows, and gift tags will save you money and you'll be well prepared for the next holiday season.

TOOLS #7

INSIDE DECORATIONS

Window Lights

It is best to keep all your lights together. I keep mine in a long see-through plastic tub so I can locate it easily. Collect extra bulbs just in case there could be a dead one. Make sure they are secure and won't fall off the windowsill. The manufacturer's instructions are written for a reason, follow them carefully.

"Home Holiday Tips That Can Save Your Life"

8,700 People a Year Are Injured by Holiday Lights, Decorations and Christmas Trees

Waterford, MI, Nov 18, 2007 - "Tragedy can occur at Christmas for anyone who spends so much time on gift shopping, holiday meals, and travel arrangements that they ignore common hazards around the home."

That caution is given by George Elwell, president of SilentCall in Waterford, Michigan, who has devoted two decades to making homes safer by developing innovative, high-tech alert products. Elwell points out that each year hospital ERs treat some 8,700 people for injuries related to holiday lights, decorations and Christmas trees. In fact, the U.S. Fire Administration reports that each year fires during the holiday season cause more than $930 million in property damage.

'There are common sense safety tips that are readily available from fire departments and safety associations that, if followed, would save many lives, avoid needless injuries, and make Christmas a happy and safe time for all,' stresses Elwell. 'But we seem to get so busy during the holidays we aren't as cautious as we should be.'

Among common holiday hazards are:

- Misuse of extension cords, both indoors and out
- Too many lights on a tree
- Worn light strands and cords
- Dried out trees
- Holiday candles
- Wrapping paper

'The real tragedy, though, is that people don't need to die or be injured when a fire strikes during the holidays or any other time,' says Elwell. 'Tragedy occurs when occupants are sleeping and learn too late that a fire has started, or when a Baby Boomer who refuses to admit to a hearing problem doesn't hear a fire or smoke alarm go off downstairs.'

Elwell knows these types of tragedies can be avoided because he has spent more than 20 years creating, developing and improving products that use strobe lights or vibrations to warn of the existence of fire, smoke, carbon dioxide fumes or of an unlawful entry into a home.

One of the most effective life-saving alerts Elwell has developed is a vibrator placed under a mattress that goes off when receiving a signal from a smoke or fire detector. The products were designed for the hard-of-hearing such as the growing Baby Boomer generation, and for the deaf or deaf-blind. Products also alert individuals that the phone or doorbell is ringing.

'When we are sound asleep after a full day of shopping or a busy night entertaining we can benefit most from a bed vibrator system,' says Elwell. 'It is something we don't think about but should!'

Elwell also suggests that thoughtful shoppers may want to put together a gift basket for loved ones containing such items as smoke and fire detectors and batteries, a fire extinguisher, flashlight and batteries or light sticks, a First-Aid Kit, carbon monoxide detector, second floor escape ladder, or some of the alert devices offered by SilentCall (www.silentcall.com).

All of SilentCall's products carry a five year warranty and are of such high quality that the failure rate is an amazing .01%. Their photo cell smoke alarm is powered by a lithium battery that will last up to 10 years. Furthermore, the photo cell smoke detectors are more effective in detecting smoke faster than traditional Ionization smoke alarms commonly found in 90% of U.S. homes. The system's transmitter will send signals up to 100 feet. Then, with the introduction of SilentCall's new Signature Series in 2008, that range will increase to upwards of 300 feet.

About SilentCall

SilentCall Communications provides personal communications and life enhancing systems for the deaf, deaf/blind, hard of hearing, and people out of hearing range. Since 1987, SilentCall has created the means by which hard of hearing, deaf and deaf-blind individuals can lead more convenient, safe lives. SilentCall also provides a life-saving tool for anyone in a noisy setting or outside their home to receive notification that someone is at their door or that their alarm detects smoke. Their entire line of expertly designed products is backed up by a written guarantee on all new systems. For more information visit www.silentcall.com, call (800) 572 5227 (voice/tty), or email sales@silentcall.com."

Exercise: Safe and Enjoyable Christmas Holiday...
BEING PREPARED

Have at least one working carbon-monoxide detector in the house as well as a fire extinguisher and properly working smoke detectors. Install at least three smoke detectors and test batteries twice a year.

- Use only outdoor lights outside your home and indoor lights inside. Never use indoor extension cords outside. Keep electrical connectors above ground and clear of puddles and snow.

- When connecting light strands outdoors, wrap a plastic bag around the connections and tie ends with Teflon tape.

- Examine light strings each year and discard worn ones. Connect no more than three strands together.

- Avoid overloading wall outlets and extension cords. To avoid overheating, do not coil or bunch an extension cord that is in use and do not run it under carpets or rugs.

- Never use electric lights on a metallic tree; use colored spotlights instead.

- When using candles place them a safe distance from combustibles. Place candles in sturdy containers. Extinguish them before going to bed or leaving the house.

- Do not place a tree close to a heat source, including a fireplace or heat vent. Be careful not to flick cigarette ashes near a tree.

- Do not put a live tree up too early or leave it up for longer than two weeks. Keep tree stand filled with water at all times.

- Never put wrapping paper in a fireplace because it can throw off dangerous sparks and produce a chemical buildup in the home that could cause an explosion.

- Do not use angel hair (spun glass wool) with spray-on snowflakes. This combination is highly combustible. Wear gloves to avoid eye and skin irritation while decorating with angel hair. Follow container directions carefully to avoid lung irritation when decorating with artificial snow sprays.

- Insert plugs fully into outlets. Poor contact may cause overheating or shock.

- Clean up immediately after a holiday party. A toddler could rise early and choke on leftover food or sample alcohol or tobacco left on tables.

TOOL #8

DECORATIONS

Again, make sure these are all together. Spend a few minutes deciding what you want to put out, what might be packed away or donated. You might have found when you downsized that it was time to get rid of some of the decorations. Ask your grown children if they might want some of them. If not, try Salvation Army, a thrift store, or www.Freecycle.org.

Best not to keep everything. As we grow our tastes change. What we might not want anymore, someone else WOULD love. Here is a case in point;

a colleague of mine had "adopted" an African family that had fled to the United States. He was a professor with 13 children. They had nothing and the holidays were coming. She called and asked me if I had any extra holiday decorations I no longer wanted or needed. That evening I went to the mudroom, where I store all the holiday items, and placed all those decorations, ornaments and lights I did not want into some large boxes. When I was done I had three boxes. The family was so appreciative and it made such a difference to those who had nothing.

TOOL #9

TREE STAND

If you are like me, you are crazed with the excitement to get the tree up and decorated. I still love the fresh smell of the natural trees, although, I am not thrilled with the cleanup. I have found those large "trash" bags that can go around the base of the tree are wonderful to engulf the tired tree after the holidays are over. Make sure that you cut a hole in the bottom of the bag, so the tree gets the water it needs to stay fresh. I have even wrapped a king or queen size sheet around the tree when moving it outdoors.

What do you use for a tree stand? I have seen everything from a bucket to a tree inside a playpen. Yes, these people needed to keep the toddler away from the tree as well as the puppy. Pretty clever and it worked!

Exercise:

() **Green Tip:** Those little creatures outside could use some protection from the winter's cold blasts. Cut off the branches or bows of the tree and place them outside around the bushes. Small Animals and even tiny birds will seek its shelter.

TOOL #10

SUPPLIES

Here is a list of supplies that I have on hand right in my wrapping container:

- 4 rolls of clear tape
- 2 rolls of double-sided tape
- 1 hand-held one-hole paper punch
- 2 pencils with erasers
- 6 pens: 1 blue, 1 red, 1 green, 1 silver, 1 gold, 1 black
- 1 pair of scissors
- 1 pair of pinking shears

- 1 roll of twine
- 1 roll of beige raffia
- 1 spool of gold thread
- 1 spool of silver thread
- 1 roll white string

Exercise:

If you do not have room in the storage container, use a large square tin (similar to a cookie tin), a basket, or a small box. If you cannot see what is in it, label it on the outside "Holiday Supplies."

TOOL #11

THANK YOU NOTES

With technology today, yes, I have seen thank-you notes sent via emails. Personally, I rather like the old-fashioned way of responding with pen in hand, written on a piece of paper, slipped into an envelope, and mailed. However, for those who tend to be new school, you can send a politely "handwritten" thank-you note with the help from Fontifer (www.fontifier. com). This web-based program lets you create a computer font that reproduces your own handwriting, even if it is not too legible. You simply print out the template from the website, type in your "thank you" message, scan it, and upload it to the web site. You can preview your font free, but when downloading it, there will be a fee. If handwriting those thank-you notes is hard for you to do, this might be one site you will want to check out.

() **Green Tip:** By using www.fontifier.com, paper and postage are saved, as well as a tree.

TOOL #12

HOLIDAY SEATING

Want something totally different? Instead of the usual placecards, here is a clever way of seating your guests at your next Holiday event, especially if you are having a casual dinner. Collect PAIRS of cards, earrings, buttons, ornaments, candies, keys, eyeglasses, toothpicks, matches, dimes, nickels, quarters, silver balls, and other everyday items to use as placecards. Put one of each of the items in a basket or large glass bowl. Be creative. Have each one of your guests draw one item from the container and then ask them to match it with the same item on the dinner table. When they have found the same item, this is where they will be seated.

Tip: You have already created FUN.

Exercise:

() Green Tips: REUSE, RECYCLE

There is much that goes to waste after the holidays. Here are a few suggestions of "what to do" with some of it, especially when you think of reusing and recycling to keep our Earth GREENER.

Boxes

- Reuse corrugated boxes to mail your packages. All past labels, addresses, or advertising should be crossed out with a thick black marker prior to placing a new address label on it. Make sure you use a strong clear tape to seal it. Save another tree, please!

I store unused corrugated boxes in my basement to be used just for shipping. Here is another idea; instead of buying all sorts of bubble wrap, use what you might be shredding as lining to protect the gift. This is a great way to recycle!

- Save the "shirt boxes" or boxes that clothes and other flat items come in. These can be reused for next year's gift giving.

Ribbon

- There are so many different types of ribbons, but if you untie and do not tear the ribbon, most likely it can be used for another time. Again, save and reuse. Reuse a piece for a birthday or a special occasion. You don't have to use the more "tired" ends, cut it to desired length.
- Store the ribbon in a clear plastic bag, so it is easy to find the desired color.

Bows

- There are some fantastic bows out there and they can all be reused. Tear off the cardboard or paper base of the bows carefully, and then put them in a clear plastic bag to store for next year.
- When ready to reuse the next year, take a piece of scotch tape and tape the bottom of the bow to whatever it is you are wrapping. Waste not, want not!

TOOL #13

WRAPPING PAPER

This is a trick I learned from my mother. The joke was that it always took her longer to unwrap her presents because she was so meticulous with the unwrapping part.

Try this: lay the wrapping paper on a flat surface and place the gift to be wrapped on top of the paper. Measure how much paper you need to cover the gift, and leave a bit more for miscalculations. Fold the paper over the gift. Now here comes the tricky part: turn the gift vertically towards you, so you are using your tummy to hold one end of the wrapped gift. Fold the corners of one end. Now turn that folded end towards your tummy so that end is not moving. Now fold the corners of the other end. Once you have both ends folded in, place your hands on either side of the ends of the gift and turn it upright. If you have done this correctly, the folded/turned in ends will lie flat UNDER the wrapped gift. Now you are ready for the ribbon. Note: If you are using a bow, you will need to tape the ends together.

Exercise:

If you have too much paper on the ends, don't waste, cut some off and make a card or gift tag with this left over paper.

() Green Tip: Do not throw out used wrapping paper. This is a waste and it can be reused if not too terribly tired and ripped. Simply cut off the ends that look too torn and reuse. It is a wonder what a fresh bow, silk flower, or raffia will do to make it look good as new.

Cards or gift tags could come from lots of places. Be creative. I have used outdated old maps, kid's art, posters, newspapers, a collage of magazines, wallpaper, brown paper, tissue paper, stockings, baskets…use your imagination…anything goes.

TOOL #14

REUSE, RECYCLE

Glass Bottles

- It is not uncommon to see a "trash" container labeled "recyclables" at a party. This is a very easy way for your guests to help in your recycling effort. Not a bad way to have them be more conscious of what they could also do at their own parties.
- We all have gotten much GREENER. Take all redeemables to the store. Treat yourself with the money collected or donate it.
- Donate the recycled glass bottles to a bottle drive.

Corks

Here is something I learned...instead of trashing your corks, simply mail them to Yemm and Hart, a Missouri based company that manufactures eco-friendly products. This company turns corks into coasters, clipboards, and flooring. I read it takes 1,333,333 corks or 1,000 pounds of them to begin the manufacturing process. This company does offer discounts on finished products for those who donate.

To learn more about them, go to www.yemmhart.com and toast yourself.

Cans

- If you don't want to be hassled with taking the redeemables back to the store, donate your cans to a charity that is collecting. Many times the Scouts, schools, or local fund drives will be collecting them. Don't pass up these opportunities to give TWICE.
- Don't add to the landfills! Have a container handy to catch all those recyclable cans your guests might have used. Write a catchy sign on the container, saying you are "environmentally friendly."

TOOL #15

HOLIDAY CARDS

I had a client who took a picture of her kids each month for one year, then made a collage for their Holiday card. She took that one more step and had placemats made for all the grandparents, uncles, and aunts. Wonderful idea!

Addressing Envelopes

- Make sure you have all your addresses/names ready to go on an Excel spreadsheet or on a Word label document for easy printing.

- If you know of someone who is more tech-savvy than yourself, maybe you could barter or offer to trade services.
- Get your labels, envelopes, and cards ready to go before the first of December.
- Spend time each evening writing a special note to a dear friend or relative with whom you might not have been in touch with for some time. Now by this I don't mean do all the writing in one evening, I mean take five or 10 cards and do a little at a time. Remember my motto, "One step at a time."
- Why not share this job with someone? Have a child or two help you with this if they are willing to jot down a few sentences. Why not share in the experience?

TOOL #16

INCOMING CARDS

Where do you put the cards that come in? I remember while living in Holden, Mass., my parents would put a basket on the front hall table. After school, snack in hand, I would always get the basket and see who had sent us a card. Even as an adult, when visiting my parents, I would gravitate towards that basket once again. It is no wonder I adopted the tradition with my own family and watched my own children go though the same motions. Building a little tradition is a joy.

() **Green Tip:** Save, save, save all of those incoming cards. Cut out/off the picture, text, greeting or whatever it is that you like. Punch a hole in the corner and affix a ribbon, twine, or raffia...voila, you now have a gift tag for next year's gifts. Simple!

() **Green Tip:** What should you do with all of those duplicate photographs from the year? Now is the time to pop them into one of the envelopes that might be going to a relative or a friend. These are even easy to make into a custom card. Wish them the very best during these holiday times and let them know you are thinking of them, too.

Exercise: Checking the Incoming Envelope Addresses

- Make sure you save the envelopes to cross-check addresses.
- Some of your friends might have changed addresses; so it is good to double-check your list for future use.
- Shred the envelopes once you have cross-checked the addresses.

() **Green Tip:** The shredded envelopes can be used as packaging material. Store in a large, clear plastic bag.

TOOL #17

DISPLAYING HOLIDAY CARDS

Where do you put all your holiday cards? In a basket? In a pile? On the kitchen table? Affixed on ribbon hanging on a door? WHERE??

- Keep them centrally located so everyone will be able to see who was thinking of you.

- Where? ...in a basket, in a decorative box, in a ceramic bowl, in a cardholder, on ribbon, taped on a window, but don't throw them in a pile.

Now what do you do when the season is over...

Exercise:

() **Green Tip:** With scissors, cut and save the picture. Next, take a paper hole punch and make a hole in the upper left corner of the card. Only thing left to do is to thread a piece of string, ribbon, raffia, or whatever your choice is through the hole and VOILA, now you have a GIFT TAG ready for next year.

TOOL #18

PAPER SHREDDING

Why do people use a paper shredder? To protect against identity theft. Well, here is a way to use all that paper for other purposes. Instead of balling up tissue paper into a gift box, shred the same colored paper (or a mixture of colors) and use as festive strips inside gift bags or boxes. Use to fill and create a gift basket. I have even been known to shred all our paper and give it to our daughter for the lining of her rabbit's crate.

Tip: Don't include plastic wrappers, CDs, or credit cards.

TOOL #19

ALL THOSE CATALOGS

I know I may be taking this a bit too far, but it *is* something I have done in the past. If you want to do something out of the ordinary and think a bit out-of-the-box, think about the person you are giving to. Does this person like fashion, outdoors, skiing, fishing, sports, computers, technology, whatever it is; use those pertinent catalogs to wrap his or her gift. I guarantee you will get a huge smile.

Exercise:

Recycle all those catalogs by donating them to schools, preschools, art schools, nursing homes, hospital waiting areas, doctors' offices or place them at your curbside recycling area. Don't just toss them in the trash; someone else would love them. First, remove your mailing label from the cover.

TOOL #20

MAKE YOUR HOLIDAY PARTY FABULOUS

We all want to make our holiday parties the very best... good food and good friends are some of the most important ingredients. Here are some fool-proof methods to help you in planning your own party.

- Send an actual invitation. These can be some of your kid's artwork, recycled Holiday cards (with a stamped "what, where, when, time, given by whom, RSVP") or anything downloaded from the Internet. Then decorate to your heart's content.

- Do-it-Yourself software can help you out too. Go to www.Mountaincow.com, www.paperbuzz.com, www.notfromabox.com. Many of these will provide you with a wealth of elegant designs, templates for you to decorate with text, and so much more. Some sophisticated-looking designs will stand out among the rest.

- Feel free to use this invitation to set the theme for the party. Go for it, have a great time, and be creative.

- When thinking about being creative, now is the time to begin to think about what you are going to serve at your party...does the theme of the party determine what you might be preparing? Whether it does or not, I have provided you with a grocery list (Worksheet #2).

So don't be caught going through the aisles, buying more than you need; sit down with your list and buy only what you need. This is particularly important if you are on a budget. And don't forget those coupons, specials, or sales; every penny saved is worth it! You will find this is an all-comprehensive list for you to use. If you need to add special notes; there is a place just for that.

Exercise:

WORKSHEET #2, Grocery List*

() Green Tip: You may want to Email invitations. It is another way to conserve paper and save our trees.

When planning for a party, it is the preparation and the follow through that are key elements for a successful event. In the back of this chapter, I have provided you with Worksheet #3-a "Countdown" for stress free preparation and planning.

> ✓ For your own printable Grocery List, go to
> *www.SoSmartOnline.com/Clutter*

PRODUCE ITEMS	CANNED FRUITS	MEAT ITEMS	CANNED MEATS
FRUITS	_ Mixed Fruit	_ Ground beef	_ Chicken/Ham
_ Apples	_ Peaches	_ Roast	_ Corned Beef
_ Bananas	_ Pears	_ Steak	_ Salmon
_ Berries	_ Pineapples	_ Hot Dogs	_ Tuna
_ Grapes			
_ Lemons/Limes	CANNED VEGGIES	POULTRY	SEASONINGS
_ Melons	_ Asparagus	_ Boneless Breast	_ Celery Salt
_ Nectarines	_ Carrots	_ Breast with Bone	_ Cinnamon
_ Oranges	_ Corn	_ Legs	_ Garlic Powder
_ Peaches	_ Green beans	_ Whole Chicken	_ Garlic Salt
_ Pears	_ Peas	_ Wings	_ Ginger
_ Plums	_ Potatoes	_ Whole Turkey	_ Nutmeg
_ Strawberries	_ Tomatoes	_ Turkey Breast	_ Onion Powder
_ Watermelon		_ Cornish Game Hens	_ Oregano
	BEANS		_ Paprika
VEGETABLES	_ Baked Beans	DELI	_ Parsley
_ Asparagus	_ Green Beans	_ Ham	_ Pepper
_ Broccoli	_ Kidney Beans	_ Roast Beef	_ Salt
_ Cabbage	_ Pinto Beans	_ Turkey	
_ Carrots	_ PorkNBeans	_ Cheese	CONDIMENTS
_ Celery	_ String Beans		_ BBQ Sauce
_ Corn		PORK	_ Honey
_ Garlic	FROZEN ITEMS	_ Bacon	_ Horseradish
_ Lettuce	_ Broccoli	_ Chops	_ Jelly/Jam ()
_ Mushrooms	_ Carrots/Corn	_ Ham	_ Ketchup
_ Onions	_ Pie Dough	_ Roast	_ Mayonnaise
_ Peppers (Red/	_ Dinners	_ Sausage	_ Mustard
Green)	_ Cookie Dough		_ Peanut Butter
_ Potato	_ Ice Cream	SEAFOOD	_ Salsa
_ Squash	_ Weight Watcher	_ Fish	_ Soy Sauce
_ Sweet Potato	Pops	_ Scallops	_ Syrup
_ Tomatoes	_ Mixed Veggies	_ Shrimp	_ Worcestershire
_ Zucchini	_ Peas		
	_ Pizza		OILS
	_ Fries/Tater Tots		_ Cooking Spray
			_ Olive Oil
			_ Vegetable Oil

_ Canola Oil

DRESSINGS
_ Blue Cheese
_ French
_ Italian
_ Ranch
_ Thousand Island
_ Vinegarette
_ Croutons

SNACKS
_ Candy
_ Cookies
_ Crackers
_ Nuts
_ Popcorn
_ Potato Chips
_ Pretzels
_ Raisins

SOUPS
_ Chicken and Rice
_ Chicken Noodle
_ Cream of Broccoli
_ Cream of Celery
_ Cream of Chicken
_ Cream of Mushroom
_ Tomato
_ Vegetable
_ Vegetable Beef
_ Vegetable Chicken

BREADS
_ Biscuits/Rolls
_ Buns (Sub/Bulky)
_ Hamburger
_ Hot Dog
_ French
_ Italian
_ Wheat
_ White
_ English Muffins

BEVERAGES
_ Coffee
_ Juice
_ Milk
_ Orange Juice
_ Soda
_ Sports Drinks
_ Tea
_ Water

DAIRY
_ Butter
_ Cheese
_ Cottage Cheese
_ Cream Cheese
_ Creamer
_ Eggs
_ Margarine
_ Milk
_ Sliced Cheese
_ Sour Cream
_ Yogurt

ITALIAN
_ Spaghetti Sauce
_ Tomato Paste
_ Tomato Sauce
_ Angel Hair Pasta
_ Elbow Macaroni
_ Lasagna Pasta
_ Shells
_ Spaghetti Pasta
_ Vermicelli Pasta
_ Diced Tomatoes
_ Stewed Tomatoes

MEXICAN
_ Refried Beans
_ Salsa
_ Spanish Rice
_ Tacos (Package)

PACKAGED
_ Baking Powder
_ Baking Soda
_ Brown Sugar
_ Brownie Mix
_ Cake Mix
_ Frosting
_ Cocoa
_ Cornstarch
_ Flour
_ Jell-O
_ Oatmeal
_ Pancake Mix
_ Rice
_ Sugar
_ Vanilla Extract

BREAKFAST
CEREAL
_
_

PET ITEMS
_ Dog Food
_ Cat Food/Litter

TOILETRIES
_ Anti-Bacterial Soap
_ Deodorant
_ Floss
_ Lotion
_ Mouthwash
_ Petroleum Jelly
_ Razors
_ Razor Blades
_ Shampoo
_ Conditioner
_ Shaving Cream
_ Soap
_ Toothbrush
_ Toothpaste
_ Feminine Pads
_ Tampons

MISCELLANEOUS
_ Batteries
_ Cards
_ Camera Film
_ Light Bulbs

PAPER
_ Foil
_ Freezer Bags
_ Kitchen Bags
_ Paper Plates
_ Paper Towels
_ Plastic Wrap
_ Sandwich Bags
_ Storage Bags
_ Tissue
_ Toilet Paper
_ Trash Bags
_ Yard Bags

CLEANERS
_ Air Freshener
_ Bleach
_ Broom
_ Dish Detergent
_ Dishwashing Soap
_ Dryer Sheets
_ Furniture Polish
_ Glass Cleaner
_ Laundry Detergent
_ Mop
_ Scrub Brush
_ Sponges

_ Toilet Bowl Cleaner
_ Towels
_ S.O.S. Pads
_ Swifter Wet
_ Swifter Dry

MEDICINE
_ Antacid
_ Band-Aids
_ Cough Drops
_ Cold-Reliever
_ First Aid Cream
_ Hydrogen Peroxide
_ Pain Reliever
_ Rubbing Alcohol

SPECIAL NOTES:

Exercise:

WORKSHEET #3, The Countdown

THREE, TWO, ONE...................................
"THE COUNTDOWN"

2 Months ahead:

- Begin to brainstorm and check addresses of possible guests.

1 Month ahead:

- Address and Mail invitations.

3 Weeks ahead:

- Make up final menu.

2 Weeks ahead:

- Decorate the inside and outside of your house.

1 Week ahead:

- Prepare to decorate the table.

2-3 Days ahead:

- Prepare your grocery list (See Grocery Worksheet #2).
- Add items you might need that are not on the list.

Day of the Party:

- Morning...make sure that you have a good breakfast; you need to nourish yourself.
- Review when the cooking needs to begin.
- 2 Hours before...be dressed ready to go!
- 1 Hour before...put on your Holiday music, CD, and get into the spirit.
- Set goodie bags by the entrance on a table or chair.
- Set fires in the fireplaces, if necessary.
- 15 Minutes before...light the candles.
- 1 Minute before...Smile and answer the door. You did it. ENJOY!

Everything is laid out for you to make this planning easier. It is filled with what to do and when to do it!

TOOL #21

SETTING THE MOOD

Little touches make all the difference. Here is a list of some of them:

- Have a gracious and convenient place to receive your guests' coats, winter boots, and umbrellas.
- Use decorations that can last the season.
- Add a bud vase with a flower or a scented candle.
- Have a basket near the front door to hold the "goody bag" for your guests' departure.
- Have cocktails ready for your guests upon their arrival.
- Have the drinks, platters, hors-d'oeuvres ready for your guests when they arrive.

In the restroom, place a small basket of toiletries:

a. Disposable hand towels
b. Personal items
c. Hand soap
d. Safety pins
e. Wet Ones
f. Hand lotion
g. Deodorant spray
h. Breath mints
i. Kleenex

TOOL #22

WHAT IS IT TO BE A GOOD GUEST?

If you want to have well-behaved guests, think what one might look like to you.

There is nothing more irritating than to not know who is coming to your party. Be polite and if there is a request for you to RSVP, please respond.

- Make sure you respond immediately or within three days at the latest. You may respond via an email, telephone, or on a note mailed through the post.

- It is not a good idea to bring another guest along with you unless you have cleared it with your host. It is so embarrassing to run out of food and drink.

- Don't arrive early unless you have cleared it with your host; your offer to help could be a welcome offer.

- Always bring a small gift. It is a "thank you" to your host. Chocolates, fresh baked goods, fresh fruit, fresh flowers, or an ornament are always appreciated.

- If you offer to bring something or are asked to, make sure you bring it and show up on time. Someone bringing the hors-d'oeuvres and showing up when the main meal is being served is rude.

- Wear your most positive attitude when going to a party. Be upbeat and listen to what others have to say. Don't monopolize the conversation.

- It is important that you remember what time the party is to end. Don't overstay your welcome, unless you would like to stay and clean up with your friends. If you are not planning to stay and help clean up, be sure to leave on time. They would like to get to bed, too.

- Send a note of thanks or make a phone call the next day to say how much fun you had. It is so very much appreciated by the host, and it goes a long way! You would so appreciate it if it were done for you.

TOOL #23

CREATE THE MOOD WITH CANDLES

Nothing says it like candles. They set a warm festive mood. Here are a couple of tips that I've seen work beautifully:

- To create a focal point, cluster candles with other objects on the mantel.

- To create a modern sophisticated mood, consider a single straight line of candles down the middle of the table.

- Always group candles at different levels and place them in unusual places.

- To create a magnifying effect, place a group of candles in front of a mirror.

- To create an elegant walkway to your front door, set candles along the edges.

- To create a theme, use all one color throughout with the flowers, candles, linens, etc.

TOOL #24

FRAGRANCE OF THE HOLIDAYS

Don't forget that the holidays should take in all your senses. For instance, those who are visual will love the lighted candles; however, use the power of the nose to hit home for other guests. For example, scents enhance any party and will then trigger memories later. What memories do you remember due to scent?

Here is an idea: if you have a pine wreath on your door, as your guests enter they will get a wonderful aroma and they'll remember your party the next time they smell pine. Or, if your house is filled with the scent of gingerbread, that is a warm and nourishing memory.

Exercise:

Tip: Use scents that smell fresh and natural. Don't put competing scents close together. Use subtle scents…too strong may not agree with your guests and some may even be allergic to others.

Exercise

FINALLY, REMEMBER GIFTS FOR YOUR GUESTS

Here is an idea for giving a little something for each of your guests. Don't go overboard; it is the thought that counts.

- Write a little note about WHAT this guest means to you.
- Make cookies or muffins.
- Fill a cellophane bag with hot cocoa, marshmallows and popcorn.
- Give an old picture of the two of you in days gone by. Laughter will erupt!

CONCLUSION

Our lives can become overwhelmed with our careers, jobs, family, and all we have to juggle in our day-to-day lives. So if you have been sparked by some of the stories, suggestions, tips, green tips, examples, and client scenarios, I have done my job. It was my intent to provide you with the necessary tools to help you make your holidays simpler and easier.

May you each create your own traditions for generations to come. Let's again put the letter "F" back in FUN!

Chapter 10
Motivation Tools: Inspirational Stories

I want to share with you some stories of either my past clients, individuals on my teleseminar or free conquer clutter classes. These personal experiences and positive results are from those who have committed to change their clutter habits. Though each of their stories may be different, there is a common thread: it takes commitment to change one's course. It begins by trusting yourself for only you know what is best for you. It may mean taking risks and challenges, but it is through those obstacles where you conquer clutter.

Mental Clutter

This young woman wanted to move to California, but felt the emotional clutter of those who wanted her to stay in the East. Her mental clutter was of not having a job, a roof over her head or transportation. She worked long and hard researching her options, making hard choices only to see her goals, passion and vision come to fruition.

Here are her remarks:

"Sallie was there to help me when I needed it. Her help has allowed me to move to the place of my dreams in my life mentally and literally. I had a dream for several years to live in Napa Valley, Calif. and finally after years of thinking about it, I did it. Sallie literally talked me through it and helped me to realize and put into action what I already knew. Her feedback, motivation, and week-to-week talks really put so much in action. About three years prior to meeting with Sallie I had carried around a small ad of Sallie's that I had cut out from a local magazine. I'd look at it from time to time wondering if I should give Sallie a call. Deep down I knew if I called her that would mean I end up living out my dream and that scared me. I was afraid to take that leap out of the comfortable state in my life and into what I loved and dreamed of over and over again. Why did it take me so long I'll never know. Now a year and half later after having moved here to Napa Valley, I am unbelievably excited and loving every minute of it. I have a very successful career in the world of Social Media for a winery, have continued to build my photography client base with very prestigious wineries, and have so many new friends throughout the valley. If I were to offer any advice to someone reading this, I would say go with what is in your heart. Sallie always reminded me to think of it as "what speaks to your heart." How does this affect your body's response? Listen to your body, your heart, and go with your intuition. When I have ups and downs (because everyone does) I often think of my accomplishments and where I came from. I remember to

believe in myself and stay in line with my goals and dreams. The more you believe in yourself, the more you find the positive, the more the world opens up for you with very little effort. You can do anything you put your mind to. Sallie was the person that inspired me, gave me courage, and held my hand through the process. She's a friend, a wonderful person, and a great mentor both spiritually and in my career. Thank you Sallie :)"

~CA

Physical Clutter

"Marsha" has worked for months to clear out her apartment. Every nook and cranny was filled with items. This was hording at it's best. This was a difficult task, but she began to break it down.

Here are her remarks:

"My life was so out of control, in every aspect, that I was getting critically ill from it. I was so overwhelmed that it affected my whole being…every single day. The minute I met Sallie, I knew that I would love her. What an absolute delight she is. She has a very forgiving nature and puts one at ease in a very wonderful way. Anybody else would have been shocked and baffled by what a mess they walked into but she just jumped right in, asked me the right questions and quickly rolled up her sleeves! She is an absolute saint. Sallie truly saved my life and thanks to her, I am starting to break through some areas, and know that there is hope. Thanks, many thanks, Sallie and with continued sessions and encouragement, I know that I will be able to breathe again (both literally and figuratively) speaking in 2006! In a few months or so, I expect to see a big difference.

You can expect an INVITATION to my newly, PERMANENTLY changed, habitable, surroundings.

It's a long, hard, ongoing project to CHANGE MY HABITS and my Ways but I'M DETERMINED!!!!!!!"

~"Marsha"

Paper Clutter

Linda is a CEO and university professor. She stated she was overwhelmed with many aspects of her home office, especially the amount of paper either from her profession or from her students. When she joined us on our free conquer teleclass, she wanted to focus on her paper clutter.

Here are her remarks:

"I've finished going through all the piles of paper and am now in a 'throw it!' frenzy. I keep all this stuff I want to read and then give up because I'm tired of staring at it. I've actually printed things more than once, not realizing I already had the document and it was in my 'to be read' file. Today's the day to fix that!! I feel the fury of Sallie!

After having completed the six-week decluttering phone seminar, I am pleased to report that my life has taken on a new momentum: calm, productive, effective, and almost stress-free. You have worked miracles in my life! I have been able to work through mounds (i.e., mountains) of clutter in my office that have been enveloping me for a very long time. In a few short weeks, you have encouraged and supported me to make some life-changing decisions about the priorities in my life and how to work with the many conflicting responsibilities I face daily. They are now in perspective, they are manageable, and they do not control me anymore; I am now in control!

I am one of your biggest fans (I am sure you have many) and ask that you keep me on your list for all upcoming seminars. This has been a wonderful experience for me, despite my angst about tossing out all that paper. My life did not end with throwing out unnecessary paper; it began fresh, and on track.

Thank you for everything, and I look forward to participating in many more of your seminars; after all, there is always more in my life that needs straightening out!"

Sincerely,

Linda J. Ferlaak, CEO

Conclusion

*"We must be willing to get rid of the life we've planned
So as to have the life that is waiting for us."*

Joseph Campbell

What did you learn about yourself from reading these pages that you did not know before? What stood out for you? Better yet, is there a change stirring?

Imagine you've rubbed the genie's bottle and have been granted the power, today, to live your life over again. What would you do differently? How would your relationship with mental, physical and emotional clutter have changed?

If you take nothing else away from this book, let it be the message that nothing happens in life without action. This is the most important bit of information I can give you.

For any of us to be successful in our de-cluttering journeys there are four things that need to happen:

1. You must choose to commit. (*What are you going to do?*)

2. You must create a plan. (*How are you going to do it?*)

3. You must take action. (*When are you going to do it?*)

4. You must be accountable. (*How will someone know you have done it?*)

If your goal is to clear your inner clutter, congratulations. It's that inner hard drive of old data that wears you out and tears you down along with those to-do lists we make longer than they really need to be and those woulda-shoulda-coulda's. Commit to changing that belief that you need to be the superhuman who can do it all and you'll find it easier to control what you can, when you can—in the present, not the past or the future. What is there to worry about? It's either already happened or it hasn't happened yet! Clear your mind and see what magic happens when you commit to being in this moment and this moment only, right now.

Be ruthless when you set forth to clear your physical clutter. If you don't love it, don't need it or it's not useful, it needs to go. These three questions, which take only three seconds to ask yourself, are your guiding lights. Be ruthless when it comes to making purchases, using the same three questions and be ruthless when you bring new items into the house—for everything that comes in, something must go out in order to keep the balance and harmony you've created.

It's vital to your well-being that your living space supports your mind, body and spirit and encourages you to prosper mentally, physically and spiritually. Otherwise, the more "confined" you feel in your personal environment, the more "confined" your thoughts and belief systems become. Purging what you do not need in your life not only removes physical and mental weight, but lifts your spirits high to allow the Universe to bring to you only what you need.

Finally, be kind to yourself when you're removing emotional clutter. Strive to limit, if not remove completely, any and all negative energy emanating from others that brings you down, creates self doubt or awakens your inner critic. Clearing emotional clutter can be difficult—you may find that you need to end certain relationships in order to bring more positive ones into your life. Seek individuals who have the knowledge, ability and willingness to share in your journey and support your growth. Surround yourself with those who give you the love and room to be the person you want to be, for you have all the resources within you to make this happen.

No matter what your de-cluttering goals, take tiny steps—and I mean tiny. How would it feel to complete just one task on your list? Would it give you a sense of accomplishment? Would it mend a broken piece of your heart? What could show up for you, in your life, if you started right now? This is a marathon, not a sprint. Take your time—it's not about finishing everything tomorrow, it's about moving forward, consistently, with courage and the belief that you can do it.

Whenever you begin (and I hope it's today, when you put down this book), remember to set yourself up for success:

Limit distractions

Work in small blocks of time

Incorporate the SMART goals system

S=Simple and Specific

M=Measurable

A=Attainable

R=Realistic

T=Time-Oriented

Commit to your SDAs (small daily actions)

Be Accountable!

Celebrate Your Wins!!!

Our highest goals in clearing our clutter are to reclaim our energy and vitality, reduce our stress, improve our health and open ourselves up to greater happiness than we could ever imagine. If the fuel in our tank is being consumed by clutter, we simply can't be available to the world or anyone in it. You deserve to take this time to focus on your goals, to take your power back and make yourself a priority.

Because if you don't do it, if you don't start down this road, who will do it for you?

START WHERE YOU STAND

"Do or do not—there is no try."

Yoda

About the Author

Sallie Felton, President of Sallie Felton LLC is a life coach, international radio talk show host, author, facilitator, international speaker and former hypnotherapist and deep imagery therapist. She was formally trained with Mentor Coach LLC and certified as a Professional Certified Coach (PCC) by the International Coach Federation. Drawing on all types of counseling and acting as a partner and cheerleader, it is her passion to help individuals who are either in a transition or trying to seek order and balance in their lives. Even those who are totally disorganized…mentally, physically or emotionally! Her unique approach, which is equal parts honesty, playfulness and genuine compassion, is what's earned Sallie accolades from clients, colleagues and radio show guests alike. As she says, "this is a process so let's start where you stand, right now, right here. What do you want, how will you achieve it and when are you going to start?"

Sallie excels in facilitating interactive workshops, such as for The American Heart Association, Mary Kay, hospital groups, corporations, associations and professional and non-profit organizations.

Sallie's radio 2 shows, "A Fresh Start" (empowering oneself) and "Light At the End of The Tunnel"(dealing with depression) leave no stones unturned. Asking powerful questions of her world renown guests and giving her over 350,000 subscribers, tip, tools and "aha" moments to aid them in their own self discover is one of her greatest strengths. Heard throughout 140 countries, it is broadcast live in Seattle, WA on 106.9FM Channel HD 3, on ContactTalkRadio.com and on the WebTalkRadio.net as well as through the World Wide Web.

She is the co-author of *Clutter Free and Clear: How To Take Charge of Your Time and Space* and *The Small Business Owner's Assessment Tool.* She also is co-author of several books including *Stepping Stones to Success* (2010) with Deepak Chopra and *GPS for Success* (2011) with Stephen R. Covey. Her most recent Ebook, *Start Where You Stand, Finding Your True North in the Life/Work Balance* (2010) is a "how-to-workbook" on finding one's inner and outer balance in the game of life. Though she says her book, *If I'm So Smart Why Can't I Get Rid of this Clutter* shares her own private stories of her wins and struggles dealing with the 3 types of clutter we all have. As she said, "I put myself out there; I wore my heart on my sleeve. It doesn't get more honest than this."

She and her husband, Conway, live north of Boston, Massachusetts with their mischievous Alaskan malamute, Kodi. They have three grown children.

If you want some coaching....

If, after reading this book, you are interested in additional coaching, please call 978-626-0090 or visit Sallie's website at www.salliefeltonlifecoach.com.

Sallie offers a one half-hour free consultation to see if coaching is right for you.

On her website you will find the following:

1. Free sign up for her newsletters
2. Free sign up to receive weekly eblast to her radio shows with expert guests
3. Free tips
4. Radio Archives of all her shows
5. Seminars and Workshops
6. Private and Group Coaching
7. Books and Downloads

Sallie has FREE workshops each first Thursday of the month where callers join me on a conference line to share their frustrations and problems dealing with their clutter. By the end, they have an action plan, time table and accountability. This has been especially beneficial for those who need that extra support, advice and accountability piece. It is all about breaking it down to manageable chunks.

To register email Sallie by going to: www.salliefeltonlifecoach.com

How to get your Free Gifts!

As a way of saying thanks for buying *If I'm So Smart, Why Can't I Get Rid of This Clutter?,* we are pleased to offer you some **FREE Gifts** to accompany the book.

Visit www.SoSmartOnline.com/Clutter to claim your free gifts today.

Throughout the book, author Sallie Felton offers practical tools for incorporating her approach into your life. We've selected a few of our favorites and made them available for you to download, print and try out. When you register, you'll receive all the documents in a single bundle.

Whether you have read *If I'm So Smart, Why Can't I Get Rid of This Clutter?* or not, these resources are free gifts from the author to you.

Here are some highlights of what you'll get:

- Practical Go-To Storage Solutions: a list of Sallie's favorite stores and resources for products to help you get organized
- "Honey-We-Do" List Template: Print out your own template and make progress on your own to-do list
- Holiday Gift List Template: Print out your own and get organized around gift-giving
- Holiday Grocery List: A complete shopping list for your big holiday event
- Sallie's List of Clutter Tips: A compiled list of Sallie's most popular Clutter tips
- Interview with Author and Clutter Expert Sallie Felton: Hear what Sallie has to say about her book

Go to www.SoSmartOnline.com/Clutter to download your free gifts today!

Journey Grrrl
PUBLISHING

Works Cited

Editors, "This Month's Question: How Do You Save Money During The Holidays?" Real Simple. November 2006: Pages 63-68.

Editors, "Why Not? Simplify Your Life This Month." Real Simple. October 2006: Page 14.

Elwell, George. "Holiday Tips That Can Save Your Life". Waterford, MI. November 18, 2007.

Felton, Sallie and Tara Sheldon. "Clutter Free and Clear!: Take Charge of Your Time and Space, A how-to-book to simplify your life". Sheldon-Felton, Hamilton, MA; 2008.

Hall, Julie. The Boomer Burden: Dealing With Your Parents' Lifetime Accumulation of Stuff. Nashville, TN: Thomas Nelson: 2007.

"How To Be A Perfect Guest". People. November 2006: Page 80.

Kendall-Tackett, Kathleen. The Well-Ordered Office. Oakland, CA. New Harbinger Publications, Inc.: 2005.

"Make Your Party Fabulous". People. November 22, 2006: Pages 35, 61-63.

Morgenstern, Julie, Organizing From The Inside Out. NY, NY. An Owl Book, Henry Holt and Company, NY; 2004.

Morgenstern, Julie. Time Management From The Inside Out. NY, NY. An Owl Book, Henry Holt and Company, NY; 2004.

Rich, Jason. Organize Your Home: Everything You Need to Make Over Your Living Space--Room by Room. MA. Adams Media: 2006

Rich, Jason. Organizing Your Home. MA. Adams Media: 2006.

"Why Not? Simplify Your Life This Month." Real Simple. November 2006: Page 20.

Websites

Sheldon, Tara, & Felton, Sallie, et al. "Clutter Free and Clear: Take Charge of Your Time and Space." Clutter Free and Clear. 2008. Sheldon Felton, LLC. 14 Mar. 2011 < http://www.clutterfreeandclear.com/>

"craigslist." Craigslist. 2010. Craigslist. 11 Mar. 2011. <http://www.craigslist.org/about/sites/>

"Crate&Barrel." 2011. Crate and Barrel. 11 Mar. 2011. <http://www.gotbooks.com/booksfortroops/>

"Gotbooks." 2010. Hostmonster. 11 Mar. 2011. <http://www.gotbooks.com/booksfortroops/>

"Invitation Software & Stationery." Mountaincow. 2001-2011. Mountaincow LLC. 14 Mar. 2011. <http://www.mountaincow.com/>

"Nurture." Wiktionary. 9 Feb. 2011. Wikimedia. 11 Mar. 2011 <http://en.wiktionary.org/wiki/nurture>

"The Original Storage and Organization Store." The Container Store. 2011. The Container Store, Inc. 14 Mar. 2011. <http://www.containerstore.com/welcome.htm>

"PEI – Productive Environment Institute." Productive Environment. 2005-2010. PTPI, LLC. 14 Mar.2011. <http://www.productiveenvironment.com/>

"Pottery Barn." 2011 Williams Sonoma Inc. 14 Mar. 2011 <http://www.potterybarn.com

"Products that make life easier." Solutions. 2011. 11 Mar. 2011. <http://www.solutions.com/>

"Rubbermaid." 11 Mar. 2011. <http://www.rubbermaid.com/Pages/Home.aspx>

"Silent Call Communications." SilentCall. 2011. Minnesota Design. 11 Mar. 2011. <http://www.silentcall.com>

"Sophisticated Stationery – Stylish events." Not From a Box, Inc. 2002-2010. Not From a Box, Inc. 14 Mar. 2011. <http://www.notfromabox.com/>

"Target." 2011. Target.com. 14 Mar. 2011. <http://www.target.com/>

"Tools and Topics." The Beehive. One Economy Corporation. 11 Mar. 2011. <http://www.thebeehive.org/jobs>

"VIA Institute on Character." VIASurvey. 10 Mar. 2011. <http://www. viacharacter.org/Surveys/SurveyCenter.aspx>

"What you need when you need it." Home Improvement. 14 Mar. 2011. DomainSponsor. 14 Mar. 2011. <http://www.homeimprovement.org/>

"WordNet, A lexical database for English." 3 Feb. 2011. The Trustees of Princeton.University. 14 Mar. 2011. <http://wordnetweb.princeton.edu/ perl/webwn>

"The World's Largest Swap Marketplace." Swap.com. 2011 Muze. 14 Mar. 2011. http://www.swap.com/

"Yemm & Hart, Green Materials." 2011. Yemm & Hart, Ltd. 14 Mar. 2011. <http://www.yemmhart.com/>

15901066R00127